ROBINSON
JEFFERS

ROBINSON
JEFFERS

Poet of California

James Karman

Revised Edition

Story Line Press

Published by Story Line Press, Inc., Three Oaks Farm, PO Box 1240,
Ashland, OR 97520-0055
www.storylinepress.com

ISBN 0-934257-58-2

Book design by Chiquita Babb

This publication was made possible thanks in part to the generous
support of the Nicholas Roerich Museum, the Andrew W. Mellon
Foundation, the National Endowment for the Arts, and our indi-
vidual contributors.

For Paula

Acknowledgments

Grateful acknowledgment is made for permission to reprint lines and excerpts from the following books and poems:

Californians by Robinson Jeffers, copyright 1971 by Cayucos Books. Reprinted by permission.

"The Beginning of Decadence," "A Barren Foreland," "The Cloud," "Whom Should I Write For, Dear, But For You?" and "Return" by Robinson Jeffers, copyright Jeffers Literary Properties. Reprinted by permission.

Dear Judas and Other Poems by Robinson Jeffers, copyright © 1977 by Liveright Publishing Corporation, copyright 1929 by R. Jeffers, copyright 1957 by Robinson Jeffers. Reprinted by permission of Liveright Publishing Corporation.

The Double Axe and Other Poems by Robinson Jeffers, copyright © 1977 by Liveright Publishing Corporation, copyright 1948 by Robinson Jeffers, copyright 1975 by Donnan Call Jeffers and Garth Jeffers. Reprinted by permission of Liveright Publishing Corporation.

The Women at Point Sur by Robinson Jeffers, copyright © 1977 by Liveright Publishing Corporation, copyright 1927 by R. Jeffers, copyright 1955 by Robinson Jeffers. Reprinted by permission of Liveright Publishing Corporation.

The Beginning and the End and Other Poems by Robinson Jeffers, copyright 1954, © 1963 by Garth Jeffers and Donnan Jeffers. Reprinted by permission of Random House, Inc.

Robinson Jeffers: Selected Poems, © copyright 1963, 1965 by Donnan

Contents

Preface

The revised edition of *Robinson Jeffers: Poet of California* is significantly different from the original. Though very little substantive material has been added or deleted, the text has been reorganized so that there are now five chapters instead of four, and the narrative follows a more straightforward chronological path. Also, in addition to subtle changes in wording throughout, more photographs are included and both the index and bibliography are expanded.

This edition would not exist without the dedication of Robert and Lysa McDowell, owners and editors of Story Line Press. I would like to thank Garth and Brenda Jeffers, Lee Jeffers, and the directors and docents of the Tor House Foundation for their steadfast support as well. The encouragement of Jeffers scholars over the years has been deeply appreciated, especially that of Robert Brophy, William Everson, Tim Hunt, Robert Kafka, Lawrence Clark Powell, and Robert Zaller. Finally, I am grateful to Carolyn Livingston for retyping the manuscript and to Paula Karman for copyediting every draft.

A word about citations. To streamline the text as much as possible, footnote information has been kept to a minimum. Quotations requiring a specific reference are followed by parentheses which contain an abbreviation for the book title and a page number—except for quotations from the *Robinson Jeffers Newsletter*, where only the issue number is provided. An explanatory list of abbreviations can be found at the end of the bibliography.

Introduction

Every human life is weird (from *wyrd*, meaning "controlled by fate"), but some lives seem touched by destiny in a special way. The goddesses who spin, measure, and cut the threads of existence work some lives into a richer, more variegated pattern, one that adds something distinctive to the tapestry they weave—a shot of gold, perhaps, or a pick of vermilion. These are the lives that others are drawn to.

Or so it would seem to look at the people who gather at Tor House each year in early October to honor the poet, Robinson Jeffers.

Tor House is the stone home that Jeffers, his wife, and twin sons built for themselves in Carmel, California. It is located on a rocky promontory that overlooks the Pacific Ocean. In 1976 the home was placed on the National Register of Historic Places, and in 1979 it was purchased by the Tor House Foundation. The Foundation maintains the home, opens it on weekends to the public, and sponsors a variety of programs that call attention to Jeffers and his work.

One such program is the annual Fall Festival, a two-day event that includes poetry readings, lectures, discussions, a variety of special events, a banquet, and a reception.

Sometimes the reception is held at Tor House late in the afternoon on the first day of the festival. Artists, writers, teachers, scholars, enthusiasts, and friends from all over the country gather in the courtyard for champagne and hors d'oeuvres. A classical guitarist provides background music as people cluster in small groups for conversation or wander off alone—perhaps to admire the gardens, colorful and aromatic in the brisk October air, or to walk through Jeffers' home, or to stand by the stone wall listening to the waves crash against the shore, watching as the sun goes down.

Guests can also slip away and climb the steps of Hawk Tower, the four-story stone structure that Jeffers built with his own hands. From the top of the turret you can see for miles around: northward, over the cypresses, to Carmel Bay; southward, to Point Lobos, where sea lions and otters make their home; and further inland, to the wild Santa Lucia Mountains. The eastern view is obscured by houses and a grove of eucalyptus trees, but the western view is open. Looking outward, you can see the ocean. A wave breaks against the rocks below as, not too far beyond, another is beginning to crest and roll toward the shore and another, even farther, is just beginning to swell. After that, all you see is an endless, undulating surface, iridescent in the last rays of the sun.

The pungent smell of kelp saturates the air, the wind blows, a sea gull drifts overhead. The timeless interplay among the elements is apparent all around. "Fire lives the death of earth," said Heraclitus, "and air lives the death of fire; water lives the death of air, earth that of water." What life do people live? What part do humans play in the mysterious dance that began long before they appeared on earth and will continue long after they are gone? These are the questions Jeffers asked. And we might add, standing where he once stood, what life did Jeffers live, what death?

ROBINSON
JEFFERS

South Shore, Malpaso, 1962, Sur Coast *(Morley Baer)*

Chapter One

Continent's End

For our country here at the west of things
Is pregnant of dreams; and west of the west
I have lived; where the last low land outflings
Its yellow-white sand to the edge of the bay;
And the west wind over us every day
Blows, and throws with the landward spray
Dreams on our minds, and a dreamy unrest.

These lines were written by Jeffers very early in his career. They are found in the last poem of his first book, the "Epilogue" to *Flagons and Apples*, published in 1912. Though stilted in style and clearly immature, they nevertheless give expression to an idea that was to concern Jeffers throughout his life: the unique significance of California, for himself and for the world. Jeffers thought of California as the place where Western civilization reaches its geographical, intellectual, and spiritual end, and he thought of himself as an artist called upon to acknowledge that fact and to dream the dreams occasioned by a life lived *in extremis*.

He restates this idea in the first poem of his second book, the "Invocation" to *Californians*, published in 1916. Addressing the western star, the light that guided civilization in its long migration out of Asia, into the Mediterranean, into Europe, across the Atlantic, and across America to the Pacific shore, Jeffers asks

"Where wilt thou lead us now?" From where he stood, on "the verge extreme," on the "shoal/Of sand that ends the west," the future of civilization seemed anything but clear.

In "The Torch-Bearers' Race," Jeffers compares his situation to that of a participant in a relay, where the flame of civilization is passed from one runner to another. Though each "emptied racer drops unseen at the end of his course/ A fresh hand snatches the hilt of the light" and carries it forward. "It gleamed across Euphrates mud," says Jeffers, and "shone on Nile shore, it lightened/ The little homely Ionian water and the sweet Aegean." Carried by Greek poets like Sappho, Alcaeus, and Aeschylus, it passed to Rome and from there to Europe and America, where eventually Jeffers himself took hold. In his hands, however, the flame of civilization was carried to "the very turn of the world." It reached the end of a long migration and stopped before "the final Pacific," the "huge, inhuman, remote, unruled" ocean, where the search for meaning must, by necessity, begin anew.

Many of the artists and intellectuals who came of age during the early decades of the twentieth century agreed with Jeffers. Though they did not share his sense of California, they believed that Western civilization was coming to an end. Revolutionary discoveries in almost every area of thought and expression, along with the violent upheaval of World War I, rendered inadequate many of the assumptions about life engendered by the Greco-Roman/Judeo-Christian tradition. People believed, therefore, that the tradition would have to be abandoned, or at least transcended, in order for them to recover authenticity and truth.

T. S. Eliot, for instance, spoke for his generation in his extraordinary poem, *The Waste Land*. He describes a worn-out, dried-up world that desperately needs renewal, a world where "the sun beats,/ And the dead tree gives no shelter," where the great ideas and monuments of the past have all been reduced to "a heap of broken images," and where the cities that once stood for something—like Jerusalem, Athens, Alexandria, Vienna, and London—have all become "unreal."

In describing this world, which is not so much a place as a

state of mind, Eliot makes use of imagery from an ancient myth, a fertility myth about death and resurrection that antedates the myths that have been important to our civilization, such as those concerning Jesus, Adonis, Attis, Tammuz, Osiris, and other gods who die and rise again. Accordingly, in his own desire to move himself and his culture forward, to slough the cerements of a dead tradition, Eliot returns to a place of origin. He takes, as he says in "The Dry Salvages," which is one of the *Four Quartets*, "The backward look behind the assurance / Of recorded history, the backward half-look / Over the shoulder, towards the primitive terror." And he finds, thereby, the path to recovery and regeneration.

The primitive terror referred to here is not feeble-minded fear. It is, rather, a sophisticated emotion which involves the humbling of oneself before the mystery of existence. It includes the surrender of one's presumptions and the willingness to look at life with innocent, savage eyes. It requires "a condition of complete simplicity" that costs, as Eliot says in the last section of *Four Quartets*, "not less than everything."

Many of Eliot's contemporaries found this path attractive. In fact, one of the most salient characteristics of "modernism" in art and thought is the return to "primitivism."

Paul Gauguin's journey to Tahiti in the late 1800s can be seen as a harbinger of things to come. He abandoned his family and career in hopes of finding meaningful answers to life's most basic questions. The title of one of his paintings, *Where Do We Come From? Who Are We? Where Are We Going?* (1897), reveals the kinds of questions that were on his mind.

Gauguin's iconoclastic style—which made use of bright, vivid colors along with muted earth tones, bold brush strokes, skewed perspectives, and richly symbolic themes—soon appeared, independently, in the work of the Fauvists ("The Wild Beasts"), the German Expressionists, and others. Pagan dancers, graceful in the paintings by Matisse, wild and naked in the work of Nolde, came to life in Nijinsky's and Stravinsky's *Rite of Spring*. Schoenberg brought discord back to music. Picasso introduced African masks into his compositions and shocked his contemporaries with the disjointed, almost brutal *Les Demoiselles d'Avignon* and other paintings. Prehistoric drawings found on the walls of caves were used for inspiration. It seemed as if artists and thinkers everywhere were attempting to escape civilization, to move beyond tradition, by returning to a variously defined, variously experienced primal scene. Even the work of Freud and Jung represents a desire to explore the hinterland of human consciousness, the underworld, where the origins of thought and feeling can be found.

The journey could be described as a retrogressive rite of passage. At least this is how Eliot defines it in the conclusion to his *Four Quartets*. Speaking for his contemporaries, he says,

> *We shall not cease from exploration*
> *And the end of all our exploring*
> *Will be to arrive where we started*
> *And know the place for the first time.*
> *Through the unknown, remembered gate*
> *When the last of earth left to discover*
> *Is that which was the beginning.*

Eliot, Stevens, Picasso, Stravinsky, and others were all torch-bearers, each in his own way. But life in London, New York, or Paris was different from life in California. Where Jeffers lived, having found and passed through "the unknown, remembered gate" that Eliot refers to, the fire of civilization had truly become a fragile flame. The fire that had once illumined the entire world, housed in such temples as the Parthenon and Chartres, flickered faintly in the night wind. It drew who knew what down from the mountains—shapes circling in the darkness with ice-cold, incandescent eyes.

"Here is the world's end," says Jeffers in "The Torch-Bearers' Race." But here also "is the gate of a world fire-new," the gate to a "wild future, wild as a hawk's dream."

The journey that brought Jeffers to California, as he himself understood it, began in the British Isles long before his own time.

In a poem titled "Patronymic" Jeffers asks, "What ancestor of mine in wet Wales or wild Scotland/ Was named Godfrey?" He was no doubt "a totally undistinguished man" who drank muddy beer and told tales of woe about Norman nobles, parish politics, and the hardships of life. He probably never found, except in death, what his own name stood for—"the peace of God"—and now, after six or eight centuries, Jeffers says, he moulders in some forgotten British graveyard. His name survived, however, and became, through "the Anglo-French erosion/ Geoffrey, Jeffry's son, Jeffries," and finally, "Jeffers" in Ireland.

Joseph Jeffers came to America from County Monaghan early in the 1800s. He settled in Ohio with his wife Barbara, where he lived as a farmer and a frontier schoolteacher. In 1838, he and his wife had a son.

William Hamilton Jeffers, Robinson's father, was raised in an extremely strict religious home. His parents belonged to the Convenanter church, a Calvinist denomination. It is not surprising then that, after graduating from Geneva College in 1855 and Xenia Theological Seminary in 1859, William became a minister in the United Presbyterian Church.

Despite ill health, he served faithfully as a missionary in Iowa. After returning home to recuperate, he ventured forth again, this time to camps and battlefields, where he counseled and cared for soldiers fighting in the Civil War.

In 1865, he was offered a position at Westminster College, where he served as a professor of Latin and Hebrew. In 1869, he transferred to the University of Wooster, where he became a professor of Greek. Just prior to assuming this position, he undertook an arduous six-month journey through Egypt, Syria, and Greece.

While teaching at the University of Wooster, Dr. Jeffers became well known for his extraordinary skill in the pulpit. As a result, he was called to the prestigious Euclid Avenue Church in Cleveland, where he served as pastor from 1875 to 1877.

Though very successful in this position, Dr. Jeffers returned to academia when he was offered a distinguished chair at Western Theological Seminary in Pittsburgh, Pennsylvania. He was a professor of Old Testament Literature and Exegesis there from 1877 to 1885, a professor of Biblical and Ecclesiastical History from 1885 to 1897, and a professor of Ecclesiastical History and History of Doctrine from 1897 to 1903. Throughout much of this period, he served as an associate editor of the *Presbyterian and Reformed Review,* a journal in which a heated debate about the authority of scripture was waged. He also continued his work with languages, being a scholar of Greek, Latin, Hebrew, Aramaic, Syriac, Arabic, Babylonian, and Assyrian, and a serious student of German and French.

It was during this time that the stooped professor, a widower who had also lost two sons, met the young and vibrant Annie Robinson Tuttle.

Annie was a descendant of William and Elizabeth Tuttle, two colonists who sailed from England on the ship *Planter* in 1635. The Tuttles settled in New Haven, where they established an estate on which Yale University was eventually built, and began a family line that included a number of illustrious soldiers, citizens, and statesmen. One of the more famous members was Jonathan Edwards, the Puritan author of the sermon, "Sinners in the Hands of an Angry God."

Annie was born in North East, Pennsylvania, in 1860. Her father, Edwin Tuttle, died when she was three, and her mother, Mary, died when she was fourteen. She and her two sisters then went to live with their father's first cousin, John Robinson, a prosperous banker, who lived with his wife Philena in Sewickley, Pennsylvania.

Annie flourished in Robinson's genteel home, developing characteristics that later led to her being described as "a woman of unusual beauty of form and character" who possessed "great charm" and a "finely matured mind" (RJ 6).

It was her refinement, no doubt, and her talent as a musician that attracted the attention of Dr. Jeffers. The professor was asked by his seminary to serve as a temporary pastor at the nearby Presbyterian Congregational Church, where Annie played the organ. Since Mr. Robinson was an elder there, it was natural for him to invite Dr. Jeffers to his home—a situation that brought Annie and Dr. Jeffers into closer contact with each other. In time, the professor made his intentions known. He wanted to marry Annie, despite the fact that he was forty-seven and she was twenty-five. Though Annie was surprised by his interest in her, she accepted on the night that he proposed and, after a brief engagement, the two were married April 30, 1885.

Because of the professor's teaching responsibilities, their wedding trip had to be postponed until the end of the semester. But when summer came, the couple sailed for Europe. They journeyed abroad the next year too, but returned with a difference— Annie was carrying a child. She gave birth to John Robinson Jeffers on January 10, 1887.

Robinson, or Robin, as he was called, was raised in an unusual home. His father, a tall, gaunt man who dressed in black, was almost fifty when his son was born. His mother, vivacious but demure, was twenty-seven. Despite their differences in age and disposition, they both wanted the best for their son—which meant, for them, the best education.

Accordingly, Robinson accompanied his parents to Europe in 1891 and was enrolled in kindergarten in Zurich. The next year, when the family traveled to Europe again, he attended school in Lucerne. Jeffers was only five at the time, but three things from this trip stayed in his mind: collecting a pocketful of snails in Switzerland (which he let loose on the walls of his school), seeing the portraits of Keats and Shelley hanging side by side in London, and admiring a hill called "Arthur's Seat" in Edinburgh. Because of Jeffers' lifelong interest in nature, his love for poetry, and his identification with landscape, one could say that the importance attached to these experiences was prophetic.

Something else that was significant may have happened on this trip. Many years later, Jeffers recalls an incident in a letter to his son.

One of your recent letters about the Bayrische Sprache—is that spelled right?—told about their saying "nimmer" for "never." (That is perfectly good German, of course, though not so usual as nie or niemals.) Curiously, the morning your letter came, I woke up remembering my father, when we were going to Europe about fifty years ago, asking one of the sailors in midAtlantic how deep the water was, and the man answering, "Da Kommt man nimmer zum Grunde." Perhaps he was from Munich (SL 299).

The crossing referred to had to have occurred either in 1892, 1898, or 1899. The earlier date seems possible because German would have been fresh in Robinson's mind, retained from his experience in Zurich the year before. Moreover, as the three recollections recounted above suggest, the trip of 1892 signaled an awakening of Robinson's mind; conversations like the one between his father and the sailor might then have been more significant. Whether it happened when he was five or when he was ten or eleven, however, is perhaps irrelevant. What is interesting about the episode is what it reveals about Jeffers. At a young age he was very much aware of what was being said around him. He not only understood the conversation, in German, but remembered, throughout his life, exactly what was said. He also knew enough to note the linguistic aberration. No doubt the meaning of the words made an impression too— "you'll never reach the bottom." They were certainly enough, mid-ocean, to play upon a child's imagination. How many hours might he have peered over the railing contemplating what the sailor said?

During these formative years, Robinson's own imagination provided him with the most diversion. His father, approaching sixty and looking more and more like "old Ichabod Crane," as neighbors called him, abhorred the sight or sound of neighborhood children. He planted a hedge to keep them from his yard and then, when his home was invaded by Robinson's friends, he took more drastic action. He moved his family to the country where his peace and quiet, and Robinson's seclusion, could be assured. As Jeffers wrote in a letter, reflecting back on this period, "I had little or no companionship with other children and spent much time in day-dreams." He thought of himself as "a flying man" or "an animal companioned man like Kipling's Mowgli," the Tarzan-like hero of *The Jungle Book* who was raised by wolves. "I was usually alone against the (imaginary) world, astonishing a curious or hostile people by my exploits" (SL 281).

Apparently, the arrival of a brother, Hamilton, in 1894 did not change the situation. The seven years' difference in their ages was like a wedge between them and, throughout their lives, though always on good terms with one another, they were never very close. Hamilton grew up to achieve distinction as an astronomer. He received his Ph.D. from the University of California, Berkeley and worked for most of his life at the Lick Observatory near San Jose.

In addition to the move to the country, another factor assured young Robinson's isolation. His father, a demanding educator, was determined that his son should have a thorough understanding of the Greco-Roman/Judeo-Christian tradition. Instruction in Greek began early, followed by instruction in Latin. Simultaneously, Jeffers worked on the literature of the Bible and on such things as the Presbyterian "Shorter Catechism" (which he was required to memorize). Despite frequent headaches and the rebellion brought on by intellectual exhaustion, Robinson was forced to continue his lessons. His father taught the old way. "When I was nine years old," says Jeffers, "my father began to slap Latin into me, literally, with his hands" (SL 353).

Though Robinson was a precocious student and a voracious reader, his progress, in his father's eyes, was never satisfactory. He was sent to private schools, first the Park Institute and then the Pittsburgh Academy.

When these schools failed to produce the desired results, Dr. Jeffers thought Europe might be the answer. In 1898, therefore, the family journeyed overseas. Robinson was enrolled in a school in Leipzig, where instruction was in German. The family crossed the Atlantic again in 1899. This time he attended the Villa la Tour in Vevey, Switzerland, where instruction was in French. By the end of the year he was reading, writing, and speaking in three languages, and he had acquired control over Greek and Latin. It is important to note that he was only twelve years old.

At the end of summer that year, Dr. Jeffers returned to America. Annie and the children stayed on, however. In 1900, Robinson attended the Château de Vidy in Lausanne. In 1901, he was transferred to the *pension* at the International Thudichum in Geneva (where his Greek acquired a modern accent that angered his father) and later, he studied at the Villa Erika in Zurich.

Dr. Jeffers rejoined his family at the end of the term and presented Robinson with a gift of two books: the poems of Thomas Campbell and the poems of Dante Gabriel Rossetti. This gift not only had extraordinary consequences for Jeffers' future as a poet, but it also reveals something important about the relationship between the father and his son.

The exact nature of that relationship is difficult to assess. It would be easy to say that Dr. Jeffers was a grim and overbearing father who, combining the worst characteristics of an old man of the cloth and an old man of the classroom, demanded far too much from his son. It would also be easy to say, based on the character of his later work, that Robinson rebelled against his father. But something altogether different seems to be the case. Whatever disappointment and resentment between them that there might have been, it is clear that the two needed and understood each other. Entries in Annie's diary suggest that they were "great friends and companions" (SMT 19).

They certainly spent an inordinate amount of time together—reading books, working on lessons, discussing great ideas. Dr. Jeffers was determined to draw his son into the world, where the wisdom of the ages could be found. That Robinson was an enthusiastic student, albeit overwhelmed, is revealed in an anecdote shared by a cousin. When Robinson was seven or eight he and the cousin were playing tennis. Suddenly, in the middle of the game, Robinson stopped playing and began to describe "scenes from Xenophon's *Anabasis* that he had been reading in the original that morning with his father." The cousin adds, "I remember saying to him, 'You'll soon know enough words to understand what our fathers are talking about'" (SMT 8).

Knowing enough words was important to Jeffers. He had

learned so many from his father, in fact, that people thought he sounded pedantic. What they no doubt heard when they listened to Robinson speak was a little boy, wise beyond his years, struggling to master the nuances of highly refined, even poetic speech. As a young man, after all, his father had revised his church's Psalter, which suggests that he understood the techniques, at least, of poetic composition. As he grew older, Dr. Jeffers "developed striking gifts as a preacher" and "the prominent laymen of the city followed him to the different churches" just to hear him speak. He also distinguished himself as a teacher. According to Dr. James Kelso, a colleague at the seminary, Dr. Jeffers was known for his remarkable command of the purest and most forceful English. "While he was slow of utterance, he never gave the impression that he had the slightest difficulty in finding the proper word to express his ideas. There was no attempt made to heap up words or to indulge in cheap rhetorical tricks. With a very incisive style, he never failed to use the proper adjective, but skillfully 'dropped' them wherever he chose." Kelso also adds that "his clear thinking and his pellucid English were always attractive to the educated listener" (RJN #43).

An educated listener is exactly what Robinson was striving to become, and he was being guided by a father who clearly understood the inclinations of his son. This is revealed in the gift of the two books of poetry that Robinson received.

The book by Thomas Campbell was conservative, didactic, and uplifting—exactly the kind of book you would expect a clergyman-scholar to recommend. Campbell lived during the time of Wordsworth but wrote in the outmoded classical style. In addition to some war lyrics, his most famous long poem was titled "The Pleasures of Hope." The book by Dante Gabriel Rossetti, on the other hand, was still considered avant-garde and scandalous at the turn of the century. Had Dr. Jeffers been a conventional man, it would have seemed out of place in his hands. But Dr. Jeffers was not conventional. He gave his sensitive son a book that had literally been raised from the underworld, insofar as many of the poems that it contained were retrieved from a grave. When Rossetti's wife committed suicide, he buried his unpublished manuscript with her. Seven years later, having over-come, to an extent, the remorse that inspired the sacrifice, he had the body exhumed. Two friends opened the coffin in the dead of night and found the poems. They later told Rossetti that his wife's golden hair had continued to grow. It filled the space around her corpse and shimmered in the torchlight.

The book stunned Jeffers. The dreamily erotic poems, the mystical meditations on life and love and death, the narratives about women who wear daggers under their skirts or who, like Dante's Beatrice, lead men toward the truth, all kindled his imag-ination. Jeffers tells the story in a short essay titled "Remembered Verses," which appears in Sidney Albert's *Bibliography*.

> My first deeply felt encounter with poetry interests me; for it was rather bizarre, besides being one of the greatest pleasures I ever experienced. I was fourteen or fifteen, at school in Switzerland, and my father on one of his summer visits brought me two little paper-bound books, poems of Thomas Campbell and poems of D. G. Rossetti. Neither name meant anything to my mind; nor did Campbell's poetry; but no lines of print will ever intoxicate as Rossetti's rather florid verses did, from *The Blessed Damozel* to the least last sonnet. I wonder why was that? How had Longfellow's *Hiawatha*, or Horace and La Fontaine, or associa-tion football and the Swiss lakes, conditioned my mind to thrill to Rossetti?
>
> My pleasure was pure; I was never a critical reader, and was not yet looking for someone to imitate. And now, if I should ever wonder about the uses of poetry, I have only to remember that year's experience. The book was worn out with reading; when it fell to pieces I was sixteen and found Swinburne. Later came *The Wind Among the Reeds*, and Shelley, and Tennyson's *Alcaics* and *Boadicea*, doubtful imitations of classical meter but sonorous as the beat of surf; when I grew older came Milton and Marlowe and many another; normal and reasonable raptures; but never again the passionate springtime that Rossetti (of all authors!) made me live.

Dr. Jeffers probably knew this would happen. He had worked with students all his life and could gauge the impact a particular book might have. With Robinson, he knew he was raising a scholar or an artist—his love for learning indicated that. The gift of the two books of poems brought Robinson to a fork in the road. Robinson's choice, the path that leads to, as Yeats called it, the "rag-and-bone shop of the heart," no doubt pleased Dr. Jeffers. At least he knew that a choice had been made and that Robinson was on his way.

The full impact of Dr. Jeffers on his son cannot be assessed here. One can say, though, that it was deep, long-lasting, and relatively free of psychological trauma. Despite his very difficult personality, he seems to have functioned as an archetypal wise old man. Though he had his own commitments—as Robinson says addressing him, "Christ was your lord and captain all your life" (SP 71)—he never required his son to share his faith. Moreover, his own commitments changed. Despite his conservative beginnings, he was described, later in life, as "a man of liberal views, which progressively relaxed in creed and dogma" (SL 265). As Robinson himself says, putting to rest the notion that he defined himself through rebellion, "my father was a clergyman but also intelligent, and he brought me up to timely ideas about origin of species, descent of man, astronomy, geology, etc., so that progress was gradual, none of the view-points of modern science came as a revelation" (SL 255). Though Robinson knew that his father had his limitations, he also knew that, as a thinker and as an explorer, "he burst/ Many strong bonds of folly, and made broad/The beautiful steep highways of the mind" (CA 139).

Annie was good for Robinson, too. Her comparative youthfulness and her light-hearted personality freshened the air around him. A devoted mother, she was especially helpful in Europe. Even when Robinson was in a boarding school she remained nearby, solicitous of his welfare.

Looked at from a certain angle, her life in Vevey, Lausanne, Geneva, and Zurich during these years was like something one might find described in a novel by Henry James. She was an educated, upper-class American residing in one of the resort centers of Europe and supervising the private education of her sons. With the lakes and mountains of Switzerland as a setting, she studied music, took language lessons, traveled, and participated fully in all the pleasantries that membership in refined society afforded her.

Her sojourn came to an end during the summer of 1902 when Dr. Jeffers decided it was time for her and the children to accompany him home.

Robinson entered the University of Pittsburgh in the fall. At the age of fifteen, he was given sophomore standing.

The next year, William Hamilton Jeffers, A.B., D.D., LL.D., retired from the seminary. He was offered the title Professor Emeritus but declined the honor, asking to be called Lecturer instead.

In 1903, feeling that a change of climate would be good for his health, he moved his family to California.

The Jefferses settled in the suburbs of Los Angeles. Robinson entered Occidental College in Highland Park, from which he graduated in 1905 at age seventeen. He then pursued graduate studies at the University of Southern California, taking courses in Oratory, Old English, Spanish, and Advanced German.

In the spring of 1906, Robinson accompanied his parents on another of their trips to Europe and entered the University of Zurich. The courses he took reveal his range of interests: Introduction to Philosophy, Old English Literature, French Literature from 1840 to 1900, Dante's Life and Work, Spanish Romance Poetry, and History of the Roman Empire. Instruction was mostly in German, but the survey of Roman history required Latin and Old English made use of Anglo-Saxon. French Literature was taught in French, Dante in Italian. Romance Poetry focused on medieval Spanish texts. Though Jeffers enjoyed his studies, he decided not to pursue them toward a degree. He returned to America in the fall and, with his language skills refreshed, took a job translating German medical papers for a family physician.

As a result of this experience, he decided to study medicine. He entered the University of Southern California Medical School in the fall of 1907. After two years of preliminary work, he entered the College of Physicians and Surgeons, where he distinguished himself in such courses as Physiology, Embryology, Materia Medica, Pharmacology, Bacteriology, Dietetics, and Chemical Pathology. According to one of his professors, Robinson "stood first in all his classes, and was a hard, brilliant worker" (RJ 11).

Nevertheless, Jeffers became dissatisfied with the study of medicine and decided to pursue a different career. Thus, in the fall of 1910, he entered the School of Forestry at the University of Washington in Seattle. His indefatigable parents accompanied him. As Annie says in a letter to a friend, "we felt that it was better, on various accounts, to come up here to make a home for Robin, as long as we could just as well as not." Clearly, however, she had misgivings. "He has thought about forestry as a profession, off and on, for a good while," she says, but "it is hard to say what he will make out of it; if he had a little less cleverness and a little better capacity for work, his future would look brighter" (SMT 48).

In fact, the business side of forestry soon tired him. Such courses as Surveying, Silviculture, and Forest Utilization required him to think of trees primarily in terms of lumber, something he was unprepared to do.

He returned to southern California at the end of the year, took rooms in a house near the beach, and proceeded to drift, as he himself says, into "mere drunken idleness" (SL 353).

There were many reasons for this period of lassitude. First of all, the stages that a person undergoes in the process of growing up had not occurred in Jeffers at the normal times or in the regular order. As a result, his mental, physical, and social development were out of balance with each other. Throughout his early years, his mental prowess set him apart from others and accelerated his progress through school. He was only sixteen when he entered Occidental as a junior, yet he still was ahead of his class.

His body was even stronger than his mind. Because of his bookishness one might have expected him to be frail and pale. As a child in Switzerland, however, he had been called the "little Spartan" because of his love for the outdoors. It was said of him then that "he swam the lakes in any weather and climbed the mountains, usually alone" (SMT 24). Among his classmates at Occidental, he was something of a legend. Recalling an expedition to the top of Mt. San Gorgonio east of Los Angeles, a fellow student describes Jeffers' "almost unlimited endurance."

> I think at that time he weighed about 175 or 180 pounds and he could travel all day with a heavy pack on his back without showing any sign of fatigue. The most vivid picture I have of him is of a tall, loose-jointed individual wearing a very dirty khaki outfit with a blue shirt, swinging over the mountain trails with a stride that made it difficult for the rest of us to stretch our legs to equal, a pack on his back and on this pack a gunny-sack with two or three frying-pans and a coffee-pot that banged and clattered with every step he took, hatless, and bursting every now and then into a long quotation of poetry from Tennyson or Homer or some other of the great poets (RJ 10).

Jeffers participated in athletics at both Occidental and the University of Southern California, competing first as a long-distance runner and later as a wrestler.

Though he joined a fraternity at USC, he was uncomfortable in most social situations. Up until he was seventeen he had never been in the same school two years in a row, so having friends was new for him. He did his best to learn quickly, however—which led, at USC, to a reputation for drinking and carousing. "Rumor told us," a younger student remembers, "that he was so brilliant that he hardly ever opened a book to study, and that, in the evenings at the Sigma Chi house, he would keep all the other boys from studying. The result was that they all flunked out in their next morning classes, while he shone as an honor student, without any effort." He had a "very romantic appearance," she adds. "I can see him standing languidly near the 'fish pond.'" He was "a tall slender youth, wearing light gray peg-top trousers and a baggy coat, which then was the height of fashion. His were extremely so, for he belonged to the well-dressed crowd" (RJ 12). Despite his shyness, Jeffers acquired, and took advantage of, a winning way with women.

Another reason for the dolor he experienced after leaving Seattle was his lack of enthusiasm for a conventional occupation. Perhaps it was due to his reading of Nietzsche's *Also Sprach Zarathustra*, or George Moore's *Confessions of a Young Man*, or Rossetti, or the French Decadents, or any of a number of other poets and philosophers, but from a very early age Robinson thought of himself as an *artiste* in search of Truth and Beauty.

He had begun writing poetry at the age of eight, taking himself seriously at the age of fourteen and publishing at seventeen. His classmates at Occidental thought of him as a poet and assumed that he would pursue writing as a profession. He wrote while he was at USC and he wrote at the University of Washington. When he left Seattle, he knew for certain that nothing else was important to him.

Except for love, and that was another reason for his suffering.

If William Hamilton Jeffers was the archetypal wise old man in Robinson's life, then Una Call Kuster was, in Jungian terms, his anima ideal. Robinson met Una the first year he attended USC, in 1906. They were in Advanced German together, reading *Faust*. Una was strikingly beautiful and very intelligent. She was also three years older than Robinson and married. Nevertheless, a friendship developed that was nurtured by a mutual love for literature and ideas. She gave him Arthur Symons' *Wordsworth and Shelley* to read and the two spent long hours together discussing this and other essays, books, and poems.

When Jeffers left USC for the University of Zurich, he sent her an occasional note. When he returned to begin medical studies, the friendship resumed and deepened.

At this time in her life, Una was struggling to define her own identity. Several years before, at eighteen, she had left Mason, Michigan, in order to enter the University of California at Berkeley. She met a young attorney there, Edward ("Teddie") Kuster, whom she promptly married. When they moved to the Los Angeles area, she lived the life of a successful lawyer's wife—with golf at the San Gabriel Country Club, social events, even road races in big, expensive cars taking up most of her time.

But something was missing. "I lived in an incessant whirl of activity" she says of herself. "Life was opening out more richly before me every day." But "I was not emotionally satisfied" (SMT 47).

She decided to return to school. She was guided, in part, by Frederick Mortimer Clapp, a poet friend who had long been in the habit of bringing her books to read: Baudelaire, Verlaine, Mallarmé, Dostoevsky, Tolstoi, Turgenev, Gogol, Swinburne, Rossetti, Moore, and Symons. At USC, Una found the environment she needed to pursue her interest in these and other authors. From 1905 to 1910, she worked first toward a bachelor's degree and then a master's.

Her master's thesis, titled "The Enduring Element of Mysticism in Man," reveals the direction in which her mind was moving. Written in a clear, confident style, it discusses the presence of mysticism throughout human history. At the same time, it provides an outlet for her own beliefs and feelings, newly discovered and affirmed. Chapter Seven, "The Mystical Awakening in the Nineteenth Century," begins with the following paragraph.

> We have noted in a former chapter that in certain centuries, the souls of men seem to be stirring and wakening after long sleep, and tentatively trying in a thousand different ways to break through the crust of the material, which encompasses them: at such times we see men restless, troubled, striving for they scarcely know what; they begin to hear the Inner Voice but are too unaccustomed, too frightened to understand. This state characterized the nineteenth century and now in the twentieth, we are beginning to sit quietly at home in this new world of silence and beauty, to rearrange our former standards of judgment, to try to traverse this new country of boundless horizons. We realize that the only important things for us to ponder are those matters of the soul, half-veiled, always mysterious, unseizable, but, after all the only Reality that can exist for any of us.

Unconsciously, perhaps, Una was describing the condition of her own existence for, in reality, it was she who was "stirring and wakening after long sleep," "tentatively trying in a thousand different ways to break through," feeling "restless" and "troubled," beginning to hear her own "Inner Voice," and pondering the half-veiled, always mysterious "matters of the soul" that occupied her heart and mind.

Inevitably, her marriage fell apart. Her husband, trying to explain to an interested public what had happened, blamed the breakdown on Una's unconventional ideas. As he says in an interview that appeared in the February 28, 1913, edition of the *Los Angeles Times*, "my wife seemed to find no solace in the ordinary affairs of life; she was without social ambition, and social functions seemed a bore to her. Her accomplishments are many, and she sought constantly for a wider scope for her intelligence. She turned to philosophy and the school of modern decadents, and she talked of things beyond the ken of those of us who dwelt upon the lower levels."

Though Teddie could not understand his wife, he knew there was someone who could—a "vile poetaster" named Robinson Jeffers (UR 21).

From the first time they met, Robinson had listened to Una and shared her enthusiasms. His own extensive background in languages, philosophy, religion, and literature made him a perfect conversation partner. Moreover, he was a handsome man, rugged, poetic, melancholy, intense.

And Una listened to Robinson. She was perhaps the only person he had ever known who could understand and appreciate the complex thoughts he brooded on. Moreover, she was unconventional and passionate. While the fashionable women wore their hair in high pompadours topped by large hats, Una often wore hers in a braid that fell loose down her back.

In time, their casual friendship became more rich. "Without the wish of either of us," says Una, "our life was one of those fatal attractions that happen unplanned and undesired" (SMT 47). It was an attraction neither could resist.

The *Los Angeles Times* for March 1, 1913, carried the story under the sensational headline "Two Points of the Eternal Triangle," complete with disparaging comments allegedly made by Robinson's mother about the scandal.

Actually, Annie was happy for her son. She knew that

Robinson and Una were deeply in love with each other, in ways that surpassed even their own understanding.

The couple had, in fact, tried to break apart. That was one of the reasons for Robinson's decision to study forestry in Seattle. When he left, however, he carried with him words that Una had written in a letter: "I do not see how I am to live, very dearest,— I cannot see anything ahead for many months but unending blankness—How can I tell you my utter love—my utter devotion." "I am yours," she adds, "and I shall walk softly, all my days until we can take each other's hands and fare forth for those wild, vivid joys we two must know together" (SMT 47).

The year's separation did ease the pressure. But when Robinson returned to Los Angeles and saw Una again, accidently, less than half an hour after he arrived, he knew they were destined for each other.

In one last attempt to save her marriage, Una agreed to her husband's request—that she travel in Europe for a year and think things through. It was during this period that Robinson languished at the beach and drifted into "drunken idleness." All was not wasted, however. It was also during this period that Robinson put together his first book of poems, *Flagons and Apples*, and decided, once and for all, that he was going to be a writer.

When Una returned, after seven months, the future was clear. She obtained a divorce from Teddie and married Robinson. The wedding occurred August 2, 1913. Both of Robinson's parents gave their blessing. "Hearty congratulations," Dr. Jeffers wrote his son, and "my best wishes for your prosperity & happiness. . . . I feel that you have brought us as a daughter one whom we can welcome with parental affection. May she & you ever prove worthy of each other" (SMT 66).

In planning their future together, Robinson and Una decided to settle in a little village called Lyme Regis, situated on the southern coast of England, in Dorset. A friend had told them about the beauty of the place and they decided to sail in November when rates were low. Early in the fall, however, Una discovered that she was pregnant, so they stayed in La Jolla where they had rented a home. A month before the baby was due they moved to Los Angeles.

On May 5, 1914, a daughter was born, whom they named Maeve. Sadly, she only lived for a day.

As summer passed and as the grief they suffered eased, plans regarding England were revived. Again, however, they had to be postponed. World War I had just begun.

Still looking for a quiet place to live, away from society, where Robinson could write, they decided to take a friend's advice and visit Carmel-by-the-Sea—a little village located just above the Big Sur area of California and just below the Monterey Peninsula. And so, in the fall of 1914, Robinson and Una traveled north.

Chapter Two

The Cloud

The first time they saw Carmel, Robinson and Una knew they had found the place where they belonged. "When the stage-coach topped the hill from Monterey," says Jeffers, "and we looked down through pines and sea-fogs on Carmel Bay, it was evident that we had come without knowing it to our inevitable place" (RJ 13).

Robinson and Una rented a small cabin and proceeded to make a life for themselves, one which Una describes as being "full and over-full of joy." For a long time they knew no one, she says, and in that solitude they were able to devote themselves to each other, to their work—"Robin was writing poetry" and "I was studying certain aspects of late 18th century England"—and to exploring the countryside around them. "We explored the village street by street, followed the traces of the moccasin trail through the forest, and dreamed around the crumbling walls about the old mission. When we walked up from the shore at sunset scarfs of smoke drifting up from hidden chimneys foretold our own happy supper and evening by the fire" (SMT 71).

Carmel was at its best on one cold, grey day as they set off on an outing. A fleeting fog, fine as breath, bathed everything in mist. Sound was dampened in the pinewoods, color deepened. The smell of darkness rose up from the ground. Deep in the forest, following paths wherever they might lead, they came upon a clearing. Tall trees circled a fireplace (or was it an altar?) built in stone. On the trunks of the trees, "high up under the gloom of the boughs," skulls of animals were hung. It seemed as if they had found "the last of the sacred groves," deserted now, forlorn (BWJ 143).

Pan, in fact, was gone. George Sterling, bohemian poet, aging faun, was in New York. The empty grove he built and left behind, like the empty marriage and the empty home, served as one more symbol of the dissolution of his dreams.

When Sterling first arrived from San Francisco in 1905, Carmel was almost uninhabited, though many artists had sojourned there before. Robert Louis Stevenson had lived in the area for awhile, as had Gertrude Atherton. The beaches of Carmel helped Stevenson imagine the setting for *Treasure Island* while the hardy residents in the surrounding countryside provided Atherton with characters for *Patience Sparhawk* and other stories. Sterling built a home among the pine trees (with the help of his wealthy uncle, from whose business firm he had just resigned), rented three acres of land and settled in to what he hoped would be a simple, Arcadian life. In a letter to his mentor, Ambrose Bierce, Sterling describes some of the charms of his new dwelling place.

> The house is on a knoll at the edge of a large pine forest, half a mile from the town of Carmel. It affords a really magnificent view of the Carmel Valley and River, and of the wild and desolate mountains beyond them. I'm half a mile from the ocean (Carmel Bay), which is blue as a sapphire, and has usually a great surf, and I'm four miles from Monterey. Here a soft wind is always in the pines. It sounds like a distant surf, just as the surf sounds like a wind in the pine trees. In Carmel, too, the air is always mild (SB 14).

Already an artist of considerable renown, at least in the Bay area, Sterling hoped his relaxed life in Carmel would provide ample time for poetic composition. He also hoped—or at least his wife, Carrie, did—that it would help him overcome his fondness for the pleasures and distractions of San Francisco, most of which were found in the drinking clubs he frequented with friends and in the apartment he kept for assignations.

For awhile, all went well. Sterling and his wife enjoyed their isolation. But the glowing letters Sterling wrote to friends about Carmel soon drew more and more of them to the area, and it was not long before a colony of artists and intellectuals was formed. The circle included, for varying lengths of time, a number of distinguished writers, such as Jack London (Sterling's best friend), Mary Austin, Nora May French, Jimmy Hopper, Fred Bechdolt, Upton Sinclair, Alice MacGowan and Grace MacGowan Cooke, Sinclair Lewis, William Rose Benét, and Harry Leon Wilson. Since many of his friends were from San Francisco, old habits were renewed and new diversions found. Endless parties on the beach or at Sterling's home were commonplace. When Jack London came down for a visit in 1906, the celebration lasted five straight days.

Despite these festivities, or perhaps because of them, people who came to Carmel hoping to become more creative or productive often found themselves "becalmed and supine." Van Wyck Brooks felt "immobilized" during the months he was there. As he says in his autobiography, writers around him "gave themselves over to day-dreams while their minds ran down like clocks, as if they had lost the keys to wind them up with, and they turned into beachcombers, listlessly reading books they had read ten times before and searching the rocks for abalones." The decadent lifestyle had an effect on the faces of the people. Sterling himself, according to Brooks, always proud of his classic profile, "had precisely the aspect of Dante in hell."

Even so, Sterling's reputation as a poet climbed during this time, largely through the promotional efforts of Ambrose Bierce. It was Bierce who said, "I steadfastly believe and heartily affirm that George Sterling is a very great poet—incomparably, the greatest poet that we have on this side of the Atlantic" (GS 38).

Bierce and others saw Sterling's poetry as the perfect flowering of their own *fin de siècle* aesthetic concerns, which included an appreciation for highly formal verse patterns, word music, and exotic themes. Unfortunately, Sterling was a winter bloom. Like the generation he wrote for, the world itself was passing away.

The San Francisco earthquake and fire of 1906 left no doubt of that. Though Sterling was in Carmel when the tragedy occurred, he was shaken to discover that much of the city was destroyed—including Coppa's, the restaurant he and his friends made famous as a meeting place. A whole way of life lay buried in the rubble of the buildings.

Other quakes, of a more personal sort, also took their toll. In November 1907, Sterling was in Oakland for a few days on business. Carrie stayed in Carmel with a house guest, Nora May French—the beautiful, despondent poet whom Sterling admired and cared for as a friend. On the evening of the 14th, after midnight, Carrie heard Nora take a drink of water and then make strange noises in her throat. She lit a candle and found Nora stiff in her bed with foam on her lips. As the foam disappeared and the body relaxed, Carrie thought the seizure, or whatever it was, had passed. Nora seemed cold, however, so Carrie slipped under the covers to warm her. It wasn't long before she realized her arms were wrapped around a corpse. Nora had swallowed cyanide, the sediment from which was found in her glass.

A few years before her death, Nora had said, "I fancy that all sensible people will ultimately be damned." The statement struck a responsive chord among the habitués of Coppa's, and the words were written, upside down and backwards, on one of the walls. After her suicide, Sterling, Carrie, and some of their friends talked more frequently about death. They even purchased cyanide and divided it up among them. Sterling kept his portion in his pocket from that time on, in an envelope marked "peace."

Jack London went so far at one time as to suggest that he and Sterling form a special pact. London had been drinking with Earl Rogers, an attorney, for days on end. So drunk that he was almost sober, so tired that he was wide awake, he said when

Sterling joined them, *"Let us agree not to sit up with the corpse. . . . When our work is done, our life force spent, exit laughing. . . . Is it a promise? We hereby agree not to sit up with the corpse"* (FV 363).

Already, though, there was little to laugh at. London was only thirty-six in 1912, but his mental and physical health had long since begun to decline. Ever hungry for adventure, for sensation of any sort, his appetite was now beyond control. He bought large parcels of land, attempted to build an enormous home (which burned to the ground on the day of completion), conceived ambitious projects in ranching and in writing, and ate and drank and smoked as much as he could hold—two whole ducks a day, for instance, along with plates of near-raw venison. A houseboy dressed him in the morning and tied his shoes.

Sterling himself was in only slightly better condition. He humiliated Carrie with an endless series of affairs, enough so that she left him for a while in 1912. He drank himself into oblivion. He wrote poetry. And he roamed the hills around Carmel with gun in hand, killing whatever he could find. Entries in his diary record the deaths of hundreds of animals and birds.

In 1913, Sterling's life in Carmel wound down. Early in the year, Joaquin Miller died. He was a symbol of old California, a noted poet, and a special friend. In September, one of Sterling's brothers passed away. In November, Ambrose Bierce turned his back on the world and disappeared in Mexico, an apparent suicide. In December, Carrie filed for divorce, unable to forgive her husband his excesses yet another time.

Sterling stayed in Carmel for a while, all alone. But the "graveyard of emotion and hotbed of memories" (GS 47) that was his home soon became too much to bear. In the spring of 1914, he left Carmel and traveled to New York.

Despite his failings, Sterling was the kind of person that creative people liked to be around. According to Mary Austin, he was "imperfectly humanized, having the intellects and will of man, but emotions and instincts almost wholly of the wild creature sort" (GS 38). He was passionate, playful, and dangerous. When he left Carmel, he was dearly missed.

It was into the vacuum created by his departure that, a few months later, Robinson and Una stepped. They could feel it in the "sacred grove" they happened on. As they stood there, encircled by the skull-hung trees, they had no way of knowing that, in ten years' time, the absent genius of the place would play a key role in the creation of Jeffers' career. But much was yet to happen before Sterling's life and Jeffers' would intertwine.

In December, wanting to see more of the coast, Robinson and Una rode the horse-drawn mail stage down to Big Sur, where the road ended. "It was night before we arrived," says Jeffers in his preface to *Jeffers Country*, "and every mile of the forty had been enchanted. We, and our dog, were the only passengers on the mail stage; we were young and in love, perhaps that contributed to the enchantment. And the coast had displayed all its winter magic for us: drifts of silver rain through great gorges, clouds dragging on the summits, storm on the rock shore, sacred calm under the redwoods."

Subsequent journeys only intensified the spell, as is evident from Una's description of the coast, also in *Jeffers Country*.

No longer gentle now, the mountains hurry to the sea in great precipices, slashed by canyons, only seldom flattening to a few acres of possible plowland. Cattle, pasturing for centuries where they could, have left the welts of their hoof-tracks criss-crossing many a steep hillside. Canyons, gushing springs and streams, are thickly wooded with redwoods and pines, laurels, tan-oaks, maples and sycamores, and, high up, the rosy-barked madrones. Near the Little Sur River there are dunes, whose drifting sands defy any boundaries of the road. Beyond, the Point Sur lighthouse sits atop a rock like St. Michael's Mount off Cornwall. From three hundred and fifty feet above the sea the powerful lens and bellowing siren warn mariners that many a stout ship has broken up along this terrible shore, which mile after mile is jagged with sharp cliffs and narrow inlets with only an occasional furlong of white-sanded beach, inaccessible from above. Lashing waves roll in, incredibly green and blue beyond the foam, menacing and gray in storm. Color, *color* on land and sea, greens and tawny yellows, and the millefleurs tapestry. Name the flowers to conjure up the colors—blues of wild lilac and lupin, larkspur and iris and blue-eyed grass; gold of poppies and yarrow and the yellow lupin, wild pansies and wall-flowers; and white heather, white wild lilac, candle-white yucca, and sometimes snow-on-the-mountain. Flashing bird-wings too, red-winged blackbirds and golden finches, blue jays and hummingbirds, darting red and emerald. And high above, arrogant hawks hover, marsh hawks and sparrow hawks, redtails and peregrine falcons. Vultures too peering down, and a rare pair of eagles. Even on sunny days there will be a vagrant wisp of luminous fog creeping like a live thing in and out of the canyons.

The effect of the landscape on Jeffers was overwhelming. He had seen natural beauty before—in the countryside of Pennsylvania, in the lakes and mountains of Switzerland, on the beaches of southern California, in the forests of Washington—but this was something altogether different, something primeval. "For the first time in my life I could see people living—amid magnificent unspoiled scenery—essentially as they did in the Idyls or the Sagas, or in Homer's Ithaca," he says in his foreword to *Selected Poetry*. "Here was life purged of its ephemeral accretions. Men were riding after cattle, or plowing the headland, hovered by white seagulls, as they have done for thousands of years, and will for thousands of years to come. Here was contemporary life that was also permanent life." It suited him.

Among the marvels Robinson and Una saw during their coach ride down the coast was an albino redwood "shining in the forest darkness." Snow-white foliage grew from the stump of the lightning-struck tree.

Jeffers was like that redwood. He too was struck by something when he moved to Carmel, something that utterly transformed him and set him apart from other men.

Later, after he established himself as a poet, friends and acquaintances tried to describe his unique appearance and demeanor. "I have never before seen a face like his," said Lawrence Clark Powell. "If I called it an animal face I might be misunderstood, but that is what it is: a big thoroughbred-animal face, like a fine horse or dog: a blend of man and beast, more beautiful than either: a sensitive, sad face, earthy but not coarse ... " (RJ 2). According to Louis Adamic, "every phase of his personality seems to be under powerful, apparently conscious and voluntary, control. Before you are with him long, you know that he is an extraordinary character. His face is thin, a poet's face, profound, not quite of this age and place, mediaeval, with strength written all over it" (AP 3).

"He is a tall man, broad shouldered, proportional for power, and spare of flesh," says Walter Van Tilburg Clark. "His hands are large, well shaped, hardened with working earth, and his face avoids handsomeness only in favor of strangely contained masculine strength and intensity." "He speaks little," Clark adds, "and that little in a very low and almost uninflected voice, though each word is exactly enunciated. A sense of great will and considered restraint dominates his presence" (RJN #44).

Jeffers had stern and searching blue-grey eyes. "It is difficult to look into them," said Edith Greenan, "for in some unconscious way his eyes look through and beyond one. When it happens, it is fearsome and disturbing because one feels so *alone* afterwards, so stripped! He seems so distant and *apart* from all of us" (UJ 11). Mabel Dodge Luhan agreed. "His eyes ... are deeper than the sea and clearly profound," she said. "If one meets his eyes for more than a glance, there is something active in their effect upon one. Something painfully alive and raw comes out of his eyes, like an unknown ray that burns the mists one covers oneself with. Mercifully, he quickly slides them from one's own, and this is a relief ... one has the feeling that he sees All" (UR 2).

Similar impressions were offered by Edward Weston, the photographer, and Loren Eiseley, the naturalist, both of whom were noted for their astute observations of the world around them. After a visit to Jeffers, Weston described him in his *Daybooks*.

I made three dozen negatives of Jeffers,—used all my magazines: and developed the moment I got home. It was another grey day, but I now realize, knowing him better, that Jeffers is more himself on grey days. He belongs to stormy skies and heavy seas.

Without knowing his work one would feel in his presence, greatness. His build is heroic—nor do I mean huge in bulk—more the way he is put together. His profile is like the eagle he writes of. His bearing is aloof,—yet not disdainfully so—rather with a constrained, almost awkward friendliness. I did not find him silent—rather a man of few words. Jeffers' eyes are notable: blue, shifting—but in no sense furtive—as though they would keep their secrets,—penetrating, all seeing eyes.

Weston was the person who introduced Eiseley to Jeffers. Years later, Eiseley recounted the episode in his foreword to *Not Man Apart*.

More than thirty years ago, accompanied by Edward Weston, I met and spoke with Robinson Jeffers on the road beyond his door. The circumstances have long faded from my mind except for the haunting presence of his features, lined and immobile as a Greek mask. I have also a rough memory that he spoke casually and without heat, of being called for jury duty in a homicide case, and of having been rejected by the defense because of the assumed cruelty of his countenance. The eyes looked at me sidelong as he spoke, not with amusement, but with the remote, almost inhuman animal contemplation that marks his work and that very obviously had aroused the mistaken animus of the defense counsel.

I felt in his presence almost as if I stood before another and nobler species of man whose moods and ways would remain . . . inscrutable to me . . . . In later and more mature years I have met cleverer vocalizers and more ingenious intellects, but I have never again encountered a man who, in one brief meeting, left me with so strong an impression that I had been speaking with someone out of time, an oracle who would presently withdraw among the nearby stones and pinewood.

Jeffers had always been different from others, but in Carmel something happened that exaggerated the differences. What was the source of the lightning that struck him?

Whatever it was, it came from a cloud that settled over him soon after he moved to Carmel. Despite the beauty of the landscape, despite his rich and satisfying life with Una, a stormy gloom oppressed him. As he says in a poem titled "The Cloud," which was written during this period, nothing could make it dissipate, not even his own counter-strikes.

> *Though sudden lightnings of my spirit have driven*
> *Lances into its gulf-dark womb, or glowed*
> *Through its thin flank; yet shutting me from heaven*
> *And love and my own soul, that weary cloud*
> *Has not been moved; never; nor now is it shaken,*
> *Though the hills laugh April green, and the waters awaken.*

The cloud condensed, in part, from a feeling of failure. Jeffers was twenty-seven when he arrived in Carmel—older, he knew, than Keats when he died—and he was painfully aware that he had not written anything of lasting value.

His first book of poems, which he paid to have published, had failed to attract readers. His mother used the word "dainty" to describe the love lyrics found in *Flagons and Apples*, hardly the praise a serious young poet would want to receive, while his father said of his son's work, "he will do a great deal better later on" (SMT 58). Jeffers himself lost interest in the book as soon as it was printed.

A thorough study of modern poetry convinced him that he could not follow the paths that others had taken. So, as he writes in the foreword to *Roan Stallion*, looking back at this period, he felt "doomed to go on imitating dead men" unless "an impossible wind" should blow him "emotions or ideas, or a point of view, or even mere rhythms" that other poets had not yet discovered.

His turmoil was exacerbated by news he received in the middle of December—his father had suffered a stroke and was in a coma. Robinson and Una hurried to Pasadena, where Dr. and Mrs. Jeffers were living at the time, but Dr. Jeffers never regained consciousness and died December 20, 1914, two days after they arrived. The death of his father reawakened Jeffers' grief for the loss of his daughter earlier that year. Having lost "the fair and firstling fruit" and then "the root" of his life, as he says in "The Year of Mourning," he felt broken and alone.

In that same poem he refers to his father as "the better part" of his own "diminished heart" and acknowledges the many gifts his father gave him, not the least of which were "wise counsel and sweet love." In particular, Jeffers refers to the extraordinary breadth of vision his father provided, especially in regard to poetry.

> *He patient with me planted in my soul*
> *Grave words of elder wisdom, and winged lines*
> *Of deathless verse, the seeds of living fire*
> *Struck from no recent lyre.*

The classical education provided by his father set Jeffers' literary standards very high, as high as they could possibly be. Now, with his father's passing, Jeffers was all the more aware of his own shortcomings.

According to the terms of Dr. Jeffers' will, a trust was established that would provide his wife and each of his two sons with an income of about $200 a month. Added to what Jeffers had saved from an earlier inheritance of $10,000 (from his namesake, John Robinson), this meant that he and Una could live comfortably in what was then a still undeveloped Carmel.

When they returned from Pasadena, their cabin was once again a place of refuge. Though Jeffers was depressed, he and Una started making friends. One day, while walking on the beach, they met Jaime de Angulo. He was a handsome Spaniard, born and raised in France, who sat high in a saddle and sometimes dressed like a vaquero. On this occasion, he was walking home with a porterhouse steak wrapped in a package under his arm. After talking with Robinson and Una for awhile about the two wolfhounds that accompanied him, he invited them to join him for dinner. When they arrived at Jaime's home, they were greeted by his wife Cary, who was busy in the kitchen cleaning spinach. Like Jaime, Cary came from a cultured family. A graduate of Vassar, she met her husband at Johns Hopkins Medical School where, in 1912, they both received doctor of medicine degrees. Neither wanted to establish a practice, however, so they came west to pursue other interests. Cleaning the spinach proved to be an exasperating chore for Cary so she opened the back door and threw it out, explaining to her guests that it wasn't worth the trouble. Una had been asked to fix potatoes but they were not quite finished when the steak was ready. The four sat down to eat the steak all by itself. Before anyone was served, however, Jaime tossed it to the dogs saying, "It would be a pity if *they* were to go hungry!"

Despite the eccentricities of the de Angulos, Robinson and Una enjoyed their company. As Una says in a letter she wrote soon after meeting them, "We have the most wildly interesting new friends . . . I could go on interminably about them." In addition to the fact that Jaime played "flute and oriental pipes," wrote Chinese and drew "clever caricatures," cared "for nothing but living alone far from cities" (on a homestead ranch he was establishing in the Big Sur wilderness), he had an interest in medicine and a love for language that Robinson found engaging. The two men, born within weeks of each other in the same year, talked in French and debated such things as "the merits of ancient and modern Greek pronunciation" (RJN #56). It was as a linguist, in fact, that Jaime was later to achieve some distinction. He recorded and analyzed several Native American languages before their last speakers died away.

Robinson and Una also socialized with Jimmy Hopper and his wife Mattie. Hopper, a writer of short stories and popular novels, belonged to the early group of settlers in Carmel who were close to George Sterling. Hopper was a short man, powerfully built, and very well liked. Nora May French fell in love with him, but he did not respond with anything more than a friend's deep and genuine affection. Unable to have him in this world, Nora attempted to bring him with her into the next. Just before her suicide, she fixed a sandwich for Hopper laced with cyanide. With trembling hands she brought it to the table at Sterling's home, but in her nervousness, dropped it on the floor. Carrie's hapless dog, Skeet, snatched the scraps, consumed them quickly, went into convulsions, and died. After Nora killed herself, Hopper left Carmel for five years, returning to remain more or less permanently in 1913.

During his lifetime, Hopper published over four hundred stories in magazines like *Collier's* and *The Saturday Evening Post*. One of his early books, *9009*, exposed the dehumanizing effects of America's penal system. It was written in collaboration with Fred Bechdolt, another friend of Sterling's and an early resident of Carmel.

Bechdolt, known as an adventurer (having prospected in Alaska and Death Valley), enjoyed success as a writer of books and stories about the western frontier. He and his wife Adele befriended Robinson and Una, making sure they were included in the various gatherings that brought members of the Carmel community together.

Jeffers himself was beginning to establish himself as a writer. *Californians* appeared in October 1916. This was his first book accepted by a genuine publisher, Macmillan, which should have made him happy. But he was not satisfied with the poems the book contained. Insofar as they employed rhythms, rhyme schemes, and other formal devices borrowed from antiquated poets, he knew they lacked distinction. For the most part, the handful of critics who reviewed the book agreed. Jeffers also knew, however, as one of the poems attests, that he was moving forward on some "undiscovered" yet "predetermined" path. He felt called to his vocation, as one "who receives/ An impulse or a promise from on high." Accordingly, he dismissed the poems contained in *Californians* even as he wrote them. As he says in "Ode on Human Destinies," the last poem of the collection, "Untimely thoughts" and "a theme not yet mature/ Are mine." "But," he adds, "if occasion yields me space/ In any future days,/ Or truce of storm, I shall not fail to speak/ In full" what now appears in verse that is "unworthy and weak."

The birth of twin sons in November 1916 lifted his spirits, but in the aftermath of that birth something happened which caused even more distress.

The delivery occurred in Pasadena. Robinson and Una had returned there six months before so they could be near their trusted family physician. They stayed with Jeffers' mother, in whose home Una could receive loving help and care. After the delivery, when it was clear that Una and the twins were fine, Jeffers came back to Carmel in order to find a home large enough for his new family. From January to March of 1917 he lived there alone. It was during this time, it seems, that Jeffers had an affair, perhaps several.

That he was predisposed toward this behavior is suggested by a line in one of his poems. Referring to his early years of manhood in "The Truce and the Peace," he admits to "wasting on women's bodies wealth of love." In "To His Father," reflecting on his wildness, he speaks of living through "years nailed up like dripping panther hides/For trophies on a savage temple wall."

In Carmel, it is likely that Jeffers met several women who reinforced his need to live without constraints. Evidence for this is found, as William Everson argues in his introduction to *Brides of the South Wind*, in two early poems written about this period in his life. The first is titled "Fauna" and the second "Mal Paso Bridge."

"Fauna" follows the format of a Theocritan idyll. As the poem begins, a young man bewails the passion he feels for a woman he cannot have. For whatever reason, his code of honor prevents him from pursuing her. Thinking he is alone on the seashore, by the mouth of the Carmel River, he pours out his soul to the elements. He is overheard, however, by a woman who is hiding behind a rock. When she makes herself known, she scorns his hesitation, saying that true desire should never be checked. She then offers herself as an outlet for his ardor. After hesitating for a moment, the young man succumbs to the temptation, and then finds that Venus, the mother of love, has blessed the union. The goddess appears, accompanied by music, and assures the young man that where passion is concerned codes of honor should never be observed. As if released from prison, the young man pursues and then possesses the original woman of his dreams.

Though it seems likely that the incidents referred to in "Fauna" are autobiographical, it is impossible to say so for sure. "Mal Paso Bridge," however, seems more openly personal.

In this poem, Jeffers speaks of riding northward along the

coast, between the Santa Lucia hills and the sea. Passing Garapatas Canyon and then Soberanes, he arrives at Mal Paso Bridge, under which he sees a beautiful dark woman with a child. "I trembled," he says, "when she turned her eyes upon me." Addressing her as "turbulent loveliness," he asks, in retrospect, "did you know then,/ Or only a fortnight later the full storm/ Of male desire?" She was, he says, "the shallow creek-mouth/ The surf of all my seas converged upon." "Dark pearl," he calls her, after nights of love-making in the open air, "rose of the hills, star of the sea." "Dark star," he says, "angel of hell, I am mad for your body,/ I am sick for the smell of your hair."

In addition to sex, death was on Jeffers' mind during this time. Germany had resumed unrestricted submarine warfare in February 1917, while Jeffers was alone, and this, along with an escalation of hostility in general, seemed to mark the end of European civilization, or at least the demise of the values for which it stood. In such a world, where anything was possible, "Mal Paso Bridge" seems to say, why not make love? Why not break barriers? Why not destroy what you believe in? From the violence of winter come the violets of spring.

The conjunction of Eros and Thanatos at this time in Jeffers' life, coursing through him at full force, certainly disrupted his marriage. When Una returned in March it was to a husband at loose ends. But the recklessness of his behavior along with the intensity of his emotions released creative energy that marked the true beginning of his life as a poet. As he says in "Mal Paso Bridge," affirming his new awareness of personal and artistic freedom, "I swore to drink wine while I could,/ Love where I pleased, and feed my eyes/ With Santa Lucian sea-beauty, and moreover/ To shear the rhyme-tassels from verse." Along with Ezra Pound and other members of the modernist movement, faced with the breakdown of all that they held dear, Jeffers realized it was time to "make it new."

Una accommodated herself to Jeffers' self-assertion—she understood the place of independence in an artist's life—but at a price. Throughout their subsequent years together, in what was truly a star-crossed marriage, she was intensely jealous. Many women, some for cause and others not, became the object of her wrath. In one tragic incident, later to be discussed, her anger was even turned against herself.

Though Jeffers was independent, he was not completely free. When America declared war on Germany in April of 1917, he wanted to enlist. But Una would not let him. Mention is made of this in a letter written by Una to a friend, a letter which is also interesting for the description it provides of social life in Carmel.

We hear nothing but War and "your bit" even here. Robin gets into a regular fever to go sometimes. If I encouraged him at all he'd away to an aviation school, but I can't bring myself to— yet. It is hard to face the thought of being alone after the years of intimate companionship we've had together—still I hate to keep him from anything that would be as wonderful for him as that. If I were a man I'd *have* to go.

We don't go out much—a dinner party now and again. The Bechdolts are very great friends of ours. Jaime de Angulo has a commission in a medical corps. *She* has a friend staying the winter with her. She is the sort of woman who enjoys women friends and housemates—well, so do I!

We went to an amusing dinner party there at Bechdolts' the other night. The Jimmy Hoppers were there and the Lloyd Osbornes. He, you know, is Stevenson's step-son. They live part the year at an interesting country place they have near Gilroy— the other part in New York, London and Paris. They were in France and London last winter—Jimmy Hopper has been two years at the front and left here last week on his way to France again for Colliers. Lots of war talk. No end of interesting people here.—The other night when we were dressing for the dinner Robin said 'What to wear?' and I said his good looking riding suit—and I'd wear a dinner gown. People dress so queerly here—one of us would be fixed right—sure enough.—Osborne big and grey and massively English was in golf clothes—she, his young second wife in a black chiffon velvet cut very low with Paris written all over it.

Some weeks ago we went to (a big) dinner at the Hoppers served in the garden—the Hoppers have George Sterling's house. The pièce de résistance was *mussels* which the Wilson's chef prepared right before our eyes over an outdoor fireplace. The Wilsons are the *Harry Leon Wilsons*—you know his magazine stories. They have a big place down the coast—a chef, gardeners, chauffeurs, outdoor swimming pool and that kind of thing. Mrs. W. is stunning—to look at—stunning *interesting* clothes.—His first wife is Rose O'Neil—the Kewpie creator you know—). Everyone here has ex-es so I am quite unnoticed about that—anyway no-one knows it I guess (RJN #56).

Though the landscape around Carmel was wild in 1917, when Una's letter was written, it is clear that many of the people who lived there were accustomed to the finer things in life. By this time, in fact, Carmel was in the process of becoming an affluent community. Most of the residents were wealthy, educated, or artistic; often, they were all three.

As such, they could afford to disengage themselves from the affairs of the world—but not by coming to Carmel. The smallness of the community, along with its isolation, produced an intensification of existence, especially for Robinson and Una and the artist-intellectuals they moved among. Few Americans, for instance, had the opportunity to talk with a correspondent about World War I as it was being fought, and even fewer with a correspondent of Hopper's sort. Having been born in France, he was bilingual, which meant his stories stemmed from intimate contact with the soldiers and the people.

Despite the light-hearted tone of Una's letter, she and Robinson were seriously at odds over his desire to join the service. He attempted to enlist and then, bowing to Una's pressure, requested a deferral. As a result of the turmoil caused by their disagreement, Jeffers' nerves, as he himself says, "quite went to pieces" (RJN #47).

Eventually, Una acquiesced. Jeffers tried to join the air corps but was told he was too old, at thirty-one, to be a pilot. He then volunteered for service in the balloon division. Before he was called, however, Armistice was declared—on November 11, 1918.

Jeffers would not have made a good soldier. Despite his training in medical school, training that might have helped him place some distance between himself and the injuries of others, Jeffers was unusually sensitive. He neither hunted nor fished because he did not want to inflict pain on living things.

And pain is what World War I was all about. By the time it was over, 65 million men had answered the call to glory. Of these, more than half were killed, wounded, or left unaccounted for. Those who survived where shaken. When they returned home, some found ravaged countries. France, for instance, had 12,000 square miles of land devastated, 30,000 linear miles of roads and railways bombed, over 700,000 homes, factories, and buildings destroyed. Europe was a wasteland.

Peace failed to bring relief. In the months that followed negotiations at Versailles, it became clear to Jeffers that the war had not accomplished anything and that American participation had been a tragic mistake. In poems like "The Beginning of Decadence," he looked with cynicism at the role the country had assumed—that of an Empire able to shape the destiny of other nations—especially since America's leaders appeared to be either lying or blind and its cultural institutions seemed corrupt. What else could be said about the churches, for instance, that "blessed the bayonets" when the war began and "praised manslaughter in the name of the Son of Man"?

For Jeffers, as mentioned previously, World War I marked the end of Western civilization. In its wake, traditional values—like Greco-Roman humanism and Judeo-Christian spirituality—could no longer be affirmed.

Besides, life in the wilderness of California, where civilization had reached the end of its westward migration, convinced him that his heritage was founded on dreams that were without basis in reality. What did the ocean know, what did the stars care about human dignity (the other side of which is arrogant self-centeredness) or about human life in general? From a cosmic perspective, as he would write later in "Margrave," earth is no bigger than "a particle of dust by a sand-grain sun, lost in a nameless cove of the shores of a continent" and what happens on it to one species of life during one brief instant of time is of little or no consequence.

However much he may have wanted out from under the cloud that in so many ways oppressed him, Jeffers knew there was nothing he could do. The decline of Western civilization was certainly beyond his control. He could only watch the awesome spectacle unfold. Neither could improvements in his poetry be forced. New rhythms and ideas had to come to him in their own time. And his life would run its course, no matter how hard he tried to change it. As he says in a letter written later, "No man can make an invention or a poem by willing it. They come or they do not come. We can only prepare the way a little—sweep out distractions. And I think no man can make himself a new man by willing or desiring it" (SL 272).

Some conscious decisions concerning his life as an artist, however, helped prepare the way for transformation. He recalled a statement made by Nietzsche—"The poets? The poets lie too much"—and decided that he would do everything he could to avoid this charge. He pledged to himself that he would not tell lies in verse nor "feign any emotion" he did not feel, nor "say anything because it was popular, or generally accepted, or fashionable in intellectual circles" unless he himself believed it (SP xv). In this way he could limit the field of possible topics and speak only of those things that were important to him. The quality he valued most in poetry, he wrote in a letter, was "imaginative power activated by strong emotion, so that the imagination is not displayed idly for a show, but as if of necessity and in earnest, under emotional compulsion" (SL 172).

He also decided to sift his work of anything that would someday require footnotes to understand. "Fashions, forms of machinery, the more complex social, financial, political adjustments, and so forth, are all ephemeral, exceptional; they exist but will never exist again" (SP xv). They have meaning, but only for a moment. He decided to exclude from his work most of the details of modern life, especially life in the cities, and concentrate instead on permanent things, like the sea, the stars, the mountains, grass, and human passion.

As he says in "A Little Scraping," the coast provided everything he needed.

This mountain sea-coast is real,
For it reaches out far into past and future;
It is part of the great and timeless excellence of things. A few
Lean cows drift high up the bronze hill;
The heavy-necked plow-team furrows the foreland, gulls
    tread the furrow;
Time ebbs and flows but the rock remains.
Two riders of tired horses canter on the cloudy ridge;
Topaz-eyed hawks have the white air;
Or a woman with jade-pale eyes, hiding a knife in her hand,
Goes through cold rain over gray grass.

Jeffers began to write about what he saw around him. As he himself says, the landscape of the Monterey coast became "the simplest and commonest theme of my verse" as well as "the chief actor in it" (SMT 185).

The effect of the landscape on Jeffers cannot be underestimated. According to Loren Eiseley in *Not Man Apart*, "something utterly wild . . . crept into his mind and marked his features. . . . The sea-beaten coast, the fierce freedom of its hunting hawks, possessed and spoke through him. It was one of the most uncanny and complete relationships between a man and his natural background that I know in literature."

Jeffers recorded the beauty that he saw but he also recorded the violence, which often appeared in the same phenomena. The dance of death between predator and prey, for instance, became for him a compelling spectacle, as he describes it in *The Loving Shepherdess.*

A heavy dark hawk balanced in the storm
And suddenly darted; the heron, the wings and long legs wavering
    in terror, fell, screaming, the long throat
Twisted under the body . . . . The pirate death drove by and had
    missed, and circled
For a new strike, the poor frightened fisherman
Beat the air over the heads of the redwoods and labored upward.
    Again and again death struck, and the heron
Fell, with the same lost cry and escaped; but the last fall

Was into the wood, the hawk followed, both passed from sight
Under the waving spires of the wood.

As he focused attention on the natural world, basic aspects of
human existence became more clear to him. In the wilderness,
where the ties that bind a civilized psyche are loosened, arche-
typal patterns of behavior reveal themselves and primordial
emotions are given free reign.

Jeffers was often criticized for the perverse sexuality and mor-
bid violence contained in many of his narrative poems—one
review of his work was titled "Pagan Horror from Carmel-by-
the-Sea," and another, "The Cult of Cruelty"—but Jeffers
defended himself by saying that he drew his stories from events
that occurred where he lived. "The psychology of the stories was
observed from life," he says, "and in this country" (BWJ 113).

Jeffers sensed a hostility of the region to common human life.
"It is not possible to be quite sane here," he argued. The region
has a mood "that both excites and perverts its people" (SL 68).
When he and Una first arrived, news of a woman's strangulation
was still current. Her partially burned body was found half-
buried on the beach. A few years before, the feet of a man were
seen sticking out of an outdoor oven in Carmel. He had been
murdered by his lover, who disposed of the body as best she
could and then slipped back into bed with her husband.

During their coach ride to Big Sur, Robinson and Una heard
stories about the people in the area, stories which impressed
them as much as, perhaps even more than, the scenery. In *Jeffers
Country*, Jeffers describes this aspect of the journey.

> At Notley's Landing we saw the ruinous old lumber-mill . . . and
> heard the story about it. In the gorge of Mill Creek we passed
> under a rusted cable sagging to a stuck skip, and we were told
> about the lime-kilns up the canyon, cold and forgotten, with the
> forest growing over them. Here we changed horses, near a lonely
> farmhouse where an eighty-year-old man lay dying; he was
> dying hard, he had been dying for a week. There were forty bee-
> hives in rows in front of his house. On a magnificent hillside
> opposite a mountain-peak stood a comparatively prosperous
> farmhouse, apple trees behind it, and the man who lived there

had killed his father with rat-poison and married his step-mother. This was the 'still small music of humanity' that we heard among the mountains; there were only five or six inhabitants in forty miles, but each one had a story.

Jeffers listened to the stories, absorbed them, and worked them into his art. He was helped immeasurably in this by Una, with whom he was still deeply in love—despite the turbulence of his behavior and his despondency.

By all accounts, Jeffers was a shy man. He spoke only when spoken to and, even then, with reticence. Una, on the other hand, was voluble and gregarious. She was interested in everyone and everything. When she ventured out she talked to whomever she met and brought back to Robinson many of the stories that he later used in his poetry.

"From the very beginning," says Edith Greenan, "Una gathered up the eerie tales around and about the strange Santa Lucia Mountains—from the secret caves and landing places along the shore, from farmers, from fishermen, from all kinds of people." Una had "such a glorious way of coming back home and telling some small incident," she adds, "dramatizing, building an entire legend out of it" (UJ 29). "She had a wild streak in her," says another acquaintance, "and there was something curiously satisfying to her in the roughness, the violence, of these stories" (RJN #63). According to Mabel Dodge Luhan, "she adored the passionate and terrible business of living, the strangeness, the macabre, wild horror of frustrated love . . . ; and nothing was too slight to engage her vivid interest, so long as it had an edge of keenness, a flavor, or a bit of zest" (UR 17).

Jeffers himself was very much aware of the impact Una had on his life and work. "My nature is cold and undiscriminating," he says in the foreword to *Selected Poetry*, "she excited and focused it, gave it eyes and nerves and sympathies."

> She never saw any of my poems until they were finished and typed, yet by her presence and conversation she has co-authored every one of them. Sometimes I think there must be some value in them, if only for that reason. She is more like a woman in a

Scotch ballad, passionate, untamed and rather heroic—or like a falcon—than like any ordinary person.

Una was a small woman. She had long dark brown hair which was often worn in braids wrapped around her head. Her oval face had the appearance of a madonna painted by Botticelli, but there was a fierceness there that balanced the softness. Her skin was "unbelievably white, translucent, the texture of jasmine petals," says Greenan, and her eyes were deep blue. For formal occasions she might wear a black velvet gown, an amber necklace, a medieval gold ring, and a topaz bracelet. She wore simple clothes around the house and preferred to go barefoot. Always, a delicate fragrance clung to her, which was sandalwood, the only scent she ever used.

Her volatile emotions were legendary. Anger, pity, jealousy, love, and hate could surface at any time, in any order. According to an acquaintance, "sometimes suddenly something would outrage her in what she herself had said" or in something someone else had said, "and she would just slash heads off in every direction." In the next moment "she could weep with sympathy for the predicament of a friend" (rjn #63).

Once, when reading aloud in the evening, Jeffers was struck by a passage he found in a book by Thomas DeQuincy. The passage was about Dorothy Wordsworth, William's sister, companion, and muse (uj 9). "There is the most perfect description of Una in this," he said. "I couldn't have written a better one."

> She was short and slight, a glancing quickness in all her movements, with a warm, even ardent manner and a speech . . . agitated by her excessive organic sensibility. Her eyes not soft but wild and startling which seemed to glow with some subtle fire that burned within her.
>
> The predominant impression was not of the intellect but of the exceeding sympathy, always ready and always profound, by which she made all that one could tell reverberate to one's own feelings by the manifest impression that it made on *hers*. The pulses of light are not more quick or more inevitable in their flow and undulation than were the answering echoes and movements of her sympathizing attention.

46   ROBINSON JEFFERS

I may sum up her character as a companion by saying that she was the very wildest (in the sense of the most natural) person I have ever known, and also the truest, most inevitable, and at the same time the quickest and readiest in her sympathy with either joy or sorrow, laughter or tears, with the realities of life or the eager realities of the poets.

She could sympathize with all the fervor of her passionate heart.

An exquisite regard for common things, a quick discernment of the one point of interest or beauty in the most ordinary incident was the secret of her spell on all who met her.

Jeffers added, in regard to Una, here quoting Wordsworth's statement concerning his sister, "she gave me eyes, she gave me ears, and arranged my life" (RJ 28).

In 1919, about five years after they arrived in Carmel and nearly three years after their twin sons, Garth and Donnan, were born, Robinson and Una bought land two miles south of Carmel and began building a home. It was then that the lightning strike occurred—or whatever it was that changed Jeffers and gave him his voice as a poet—and the cloud lifted.

At one time they considered building a house out of the same stone used at Father Junípero Serra's Carmel mission, which was soft and chalky, "velvet-like to touch," and ranged in shade from "warm cream to *palest* amber." They even picked a name for their dream home, "Tour d'Ivoire" (RJN #56). But the property they purchased required something different. Carmel Point (sometimes called Mission Point) was a windswept, barren hill with a jagged outcropping of stone. It reminded Robinson and Una of the rocky promontories called "tors" which they both had seen in Dartmoor, England.

It is interesting to contemplate what might have happened if Robinson and Una had followed their original plan. An "ivory tower" made of perishable chalkstone and set comfortably in a different, more protected location might have encouraged a detached existence. Such a house might also have inspired Robinson to write conventional poetry, academic and highly refined. But Robinson and Una decided to lay their lives on the line, the coastline, and expose themselves to the same fierce elements that bent trees and cut inlets in the shore.

Accordingly, Tor House was built on the crest of the hill, just fifty yards above the sea. Local granite boulders were used, set in place by a stonemason named Pierson. Jeffers worked as an apprentice, mixing mortar and carrying stones. It was while performing these chores, simple as they were, that something happened.

Handling the granite boulders that had rolled in the sea for a thousand years and were now being set into place for shelter deepened and intensified his experience of life. "As he helped the masons shift and place the wind and wave-worn" stones, says Una, in a letter written from notes Jeffers supplied, " . . . he realized some kinship" with the granite "and became aware of strengths in himself unknown before" (SL 213). He saw the hardness of his own personality in the boulders, a hardness that in future years, as he says in "Soliloquy," would enable him to shed "pleasure and pain like hailstones," and he saw the coldness that would give his temperament its characteristic stone tranquility.

The kinship that he felt extended the reach of his consciousness. Already sensitive to people, animals, birds, flowers, and trees, his sympathies now penetrated the very heart of matter. He felt the grave and earnest energy packed within stone, the calm that masks the spinning atomic structure. This induced something akin to mystical illumination. "Thus at the age of thirty-one," continues Una in the letter referred to above, "there came to him a kind of awakening such as adolescents and religious converts are said to experience."

The exact nature of this flash of insight is difficult to describe—so many factors were involved and the transformation in Jeffers was so profound—but several passages in his poetry offer clues. A speech by Orestes in *The Tower Beyond Tragedy,* for instance, captures the ineffability of the experience along with its blend of transcendence and union.

> *I have cut the meshes*
> *And fly like a freed falcon . . .*

I remembered

*The knife in the stalk of my humanity; I drew and it broke; I
entered the life of the brown forest*

*And the great life of the ancient peaks, the patience of stone, I felt
the changes in the veins*

*In the throat of the mountain, a grain in many centuries, we have
our own time, not yours; and I was the stream*

*Draining the mountain wood; and I the stag drinking; and I was the
stars,*

*Boiling with light, wandering alone, each one the lord of his own
summit; and I was the darkness*

*Outside the stars, I included them, they were a part of me. I was
mankind also, a moving lichen*

*On the cheek of the round stone . . . they have not made words for it,
to go behind things, beyond hours and ages,*

*And be all things in all time, in their returns and passages, in the
motionless and timeless center,*

*In the white of the fire . . . how can I express the excellence I have
found, that has no color but clearness;*

*No honey but ecstasy; nothing wrought nor remembered; no under-
tone nor silver second murmur*

*That rings in love's voice, I and my loved are one; no desire but
fulfilled; no passion but peace,*

*The pure flame and the white, fierier than any passion; no time but
spheral eternity. . . .*

The invulnerable beauty of the granite revealed to Jeffers the
face of God, apparently impassive but deeply strained. It revealed
his own face, equally obdurate and pained. And it disclosed the
infinite energy enflaming and interconnecting everything that
exists—from flowers on the foreland to stars in the distant sky,
from the stones at hand to the hands that held the stone.

The boulders that meant so much to Jeffers were set in place
according to a design borrowed from a Tudor barn that Una had
seen in Surrey, England. Tor House had a living room with win-
dows facing south and west, a guest bedroom, a kitchen, and a
bath. Above the living room, accessible by a short stairway, there

was a loft where Robinson, Una, and the children slept. It was a small and sturdy structure (some of the walls were built four feet thick) with running water, but no gas, electricity, or telephone.

As soon as they settled into their new home, life acquired an established routine.

In the morning, after breakfast, Jeffers would write. He worked at a desk upstairs in the loft, sitting in a chair that had been made more than half a century before from timbers salvaged from the ruined mission.

Afternoons, following an ample lunch, Jeffers worked on the house and grounds. He planted nearly two thousand trees on his property—eucalyptus, cypress and pine—each of which needed watering and care. He also worked with stone. He applied his newly acquired skills as a mason first to a detached garage, then to a low wall around the property which formed an enclosed courtyard, and then, with more confidence and ambition, to a tower.

Hawk Tower was inspired by dreams of old Irish towers. Una had a special fondness for them. It took five years to build, occupying Jeffers from 1920 to 1925. When finished, it included a sunken "dungeon," a ground-floor room, a second-floor room panelled in mahogany and containing an oriel window, a secret staircase enclosed within the walls, an exterior staircase that led to a covered turret (from which one could look out to sea through a porthole from the ship in which Napoleon fled Elba), a third-floor open platform paved in marble and surrounded by a battlement, and a fourth-floor open turret. Jeffers worked on the tower entirely alone, rolling the granite boulders first along an inclined plane and later hoisting them into position with block and tackle. He found the boulders along the shore and carried or rolled them home; some weighed as much as four hundred pounds.

The tower is not only architecturally significant but also culturally interesting, for into its walls Jeffers cemented artifacts from around the world—white lava from Mt. Vesuvius in Italy, black lava from Mt. Kilauea in Hawaii, an Indian arrowhead from Michigan, fossils from Iowa, marble from Ireland, a tile from the Babylonian Temple of Erich inscribed with a cuneiform prayer to Ishtar, a carved stone head of a dancing girl from an Angkor temple in Cambodia, a stone from the grave of George Moore, a stone from Lord Byron's Newstead Abbey near Nottingham, and a piece of the Great Wall of China. Some of these treasures were collected by Robinson and Una, others were given to them by friends.

Special stones could be found in the courtyard, too, which Una turned into a beautiful, wild garden. A variety of objects were set into the wall or placed around the grounds, such as a ceramic fragment from the Temple of Heaven in Beijing, a Roman statue of a boy riding a dolphin (once owned by John Singer Sargent), tiles from the San Antonio mission, tiles from Kenilworth Castle in England, Indian mortars, an Indian millstone, an Irish grave marker carved with a cross, a Chinese statue of a fertility goddess, stone ballast from a ship that had sailed around the Horn, pebbles from the beach below King Arthur's Castle at Tintagel in Cornwall, fragments from the home of George Moore, and a piece of Thoor Ballylee, Yeats' tower in Ireland.

Tor House itself, which Jeffers worked on and expanded over the years, also contained its share of special stones. Seven pre-Columbian terra-cotta heads from the Teotihuacan ruins of Mexico were cemented into the structure, along with an obsidian sacrificial dagger, an Aztec mask, a fragment of a mosaic from the ancient Roman city of Timgad in North Africa, a fragment of a meteorite, a stone from Ossian's grave, a piece of marble from Hadrian's villa, a piece of carved white marble from the Greek island of Delos, a sculpted human torso from northwest India, three tesserae from the Roman baths of Caracalla, a fragment of a wall painting from Pompeii, three stones from an Indian cave at Tassajara, stones from the Carmel mission, stones from the ruins of Melrose Abbey and Dryburgh Abbey in Scotland, stones from nearly every round tower in Ireland, a pottery fragment from an earthwork on the Orkney Islands, and a piece of white rock from the Great Pyramid of Cheops in Egypt. Clearly, the house they built for themselves was more than a simple cottage by the sea.

A list of the *objets de vertu* that Robinson and Una owned would be similar to the list of stones. Almost all of their possessions, including jewelry, furniture, and clothes, had personal or historic value and were rich in symbolic significance.

In the evening, following the afternoon's work outdoors, Jeffers would come in for supper. At sunset, he and Una walked for two or three miles along the shore and then, returning home, they sat by the fire. While Una sewed (making the family's clothes), Robinson read aloud to her and the children. Over the years, the family shared countless books this way, including seventeen novels by Thomas Hardy, three by Dostoevsky, and thirty by Sir Walter Scott. Jeffers also read aloud twenty-four books by W. H. Hudson (the author of *Green Mansions*) and innumerable others like Bronte's *Wuthering Heights*, Kipling's *Jungle Book* and *Captains Courageous*, Cellini's *Autobiography*, Doughty's *Arabia Deserta*, Lawrence's *Revolt in the Desert*, Synge's *Aran Islands*, Llewelyn Powys' *Black Laughter* and *Skin for Skin*, and Sven Hedin's descriptions of travel in Tibet.

After Garth and Donnan were sent to bed, Robinson and Una continued to talk and read. Sometimes they would "enisle" themselves, as Jeffers says in a poem titled "For Una," and forget about the pressing concerns of everyday life. Una would drink Irish whiskey and Robinson red wine and they would "talk about love and death, / Rock-solid themes, old and deep as the sea." They would "admit nothing more timely" into their conversation, "nothing less real," and, as the hours passed, they would spend "the night well."

Jeffers never went to bed without first going outdoors, usually around midnight. According to Una, he walked the tor, "watching the stars in their courses, marking the rising or setting of the Constellations and feeling the direction of the wind and noticing the tides at ebb or flow" (SMT 148).

The sound of the ocean was ever present at Tor House and at night, if the west window was open, the pounding of the surf echoed throughout the loft. If not the surf, then the sound of the wind surrounded them. Before the trees had grown enough to block it, says Una, "a special night wind from the valley . . .

wuthered unhindered" around the house and created a haunting wail. And if not the wind, then nocturnal creatures: owls could often be heard and, on cold moonlit nights, the howling of coyotes drifted down from the valley; "once several of them raged and yelled like maniacs in our very courtyard" (SMT 87).

The rhythm of Jeffers' life was slow and steady—like the rhythm of his heart, which rose from forty beats per minute while he was writing to only sixty in the afternoon while he worked outdoors. Perhaps his slow pulse (the sign of a very strong body, built for exertion and endurance) and regular routine influenced the characteristic rhythm of his poetry, a rhythm which came, he said, from many sources: "physics, biology, the beat of blood, the tidal environments of life," and the "desire for singing emphasis that prose does not have" (SMT 152). By "tidal environments" he meant more than the ebb and flow of the ocean; he had in mind the cycles that regulate the deepest aspects of our lives, like the alternation of day and night and the changes in the moon and in the seasons and in the bodies of women.

Another source for the primordial rhythm found in his poetry, not so obvious perhaps, was fire—the fire that covered earth when everything was molten. He mentions this in "Continent's End," a poem which begins with the following stanzas.

> *At the equinox when the earth was veiled in late rain,*
> *wreathed with wet poppies, waiting spring,*
> *The ocean swelled for a far storm and beat its boundary,*
> *the ground-swell shook the beds of granite.*

> *I gazing at the boundaries of granite and spray, the*
> *established sea-marks, felt behind me*
> *Mountain and plain, the immense breadth of the continent,*
> *before me the mass and doubled stretch of water.*

Jeffers knew that he stood between two worlds—not only the land and the sea but also the past and the future. The journey that had begun millions and millions of years before when the first creatures crawled out of the ocean and learned to live on land and then, through the permutations of evolution, produced humans, and then Western civilization reached an end on the California shore. Of course life would continue on, but one vast cycle had just concluded and a new one had not yet begun. Jeffers, a bearer of tradition, a torch-bearer, was back where humans started from.

In looking forward, Jeffers looked behind—with cosmic vision. "There is in me," he says, "older and harder than life and more impartial, the eye that watched before there was an ocean," an eye, he says, addressing the sea, "that watched you fill your beds out of the condensation of thin vapor and . . . saw you soft and violent wear your boundaries down, eat rock, shift places with the continents."

Such vision enabled Jeffers to discover the deeper source for the tidal rhythm of his verse—the movement of molten stone— which he identifies in the last stanza of the poem.

> Mother, though my song's measure is like your surf-beat's
> ancient rhythm I never learned it of you.
> Before there was any water there were tides of fire, both
> our tones flow from the older fountain.

At some level Jeffers knew this all along, even before he moved to Carmel. As he says in a letter to Una, written before they were married and before he had written anything of lasting value, "poetry should be a blending of fire and earth—should be made of solid and immediate things . . . which are set on fire by human passion" (SL 16).

Robinson Jeffers 1899

Robinson Jeffers 1907

Una, 1902

Una, 1902

Una, 1911
(Arnold Genthe)

Los Angeles Times,
1 March 1913

Robinson and Billie walking from site of Tor House, c. 1915

Robinson, Una, and Billie at site of Tor House, c. 1915

Tor House, 1919

Tor House with Hawk Tower under construction, c. 1923

Living Room of Tor House *(Morley Baer)*

Afternoon Storm, Little Sur, 1972 *(Morley Baer)*

Chapter Three

Rock and Hawk

The revelation that occurred while Jeffers was building his home enabled him to see his own life and the world in a new way. The war that meant so much, for instance, became for him a moment's episode in a far grander scheme. It was an end but not *the* end. The nations that "labor and gather and dissolve / Into destruction," he says in "Practical People," are like the stars that "sharpen / Their spirit of splendor" and then darken, and like "the spirit of man" that brightens to maturity and then dulls with age and dies. "All these tidal gatherings, growth and decay, / Shining and darkening, are forever / Renewed; and the whole cycle impenitently / Revolves, and all the past is future."

In saying this, Jeffers reaffirmed one of humankind's most ancient beliefs, the doctrine of eternal recurrence. As he states in "Point Pinos and Point Lobos," the idea had come to him many years before.

> For someone
> Whispered into my ear when I was very young, some serpent
>   whispered
> That what has gone returns; what has been is; what will be, was;
>   the future

Is a farther past; our times he said fractions of arcs of the great circle;
And the wheel turns, nothing shall stop it nor destroy it, we are
    bound on the wheel,
We and the stars and the seas . . . .

Though all things come into being and pass away, the universe itself continues on. "The alternation of white sunlight and brown night,/ The beautiful succession of the breeding springs, the enormous rhythm of the stars' deaths/ And fierce renewals" sustain the universe and thus, the life of God.

In seeking ways to express what he discovered—or what, from ancient wisdom, he sought to reaffirm—Jeffers turned to a variety of myths, both Eastern and Occidental. A poem called "Shiva," for instance, refers to a deity revered by some Hindus as lord of the universe. In his masculine aspect, Shiva is changeless and eternal. Because he performs the dance of life that creates, preserves, and destroys all things, however, he also has *Shakti*, or feminine, power. As such, he/she is worshipped as the Great Goddess, Mother Nature. Known by such names as Parvati, Kali, and Durga, the goddess brings joy as well as sorrow, gives birth as well as death, appears in winter as well as spring.

In Jeffers' poem, the goddess reveals herself as "pure destruction, achieved and supreme." She is described as a fierce hawk with "empty darkness" under "death-tent wings," a wild predator who falls on our world to bring it to an end. "Nothing will escape her," Jeffers says, for "this is the hawk that picks out the stars' eyes." This is also the hawk, however, who builds from the bones of her prey a nest in which life can be renewed.

And this is the hawk that became Jeffers' muse. In a poem titled "Rock and Hawk" Jeffers describes what he regards as a fitting symbol for the yin and yang of life. The image he proposes—a falcon perched upon a stone—serves also to suggest what he acquired when the hawk-goddess-muse broke the cloud above him, circled down, and gripped the granite of his soul.

    bright power, dark peace;
    Fierce consciousness joined with final
    Disinterestedness;

Life with calm death; the falcon's
Realist eyes and act
Married to the massive

Mysticism of stone . . . .

The first major poem written under her tutelage was a long narrative called *Tamar*. The story concerns a young woman who lives with her family in an isolated farmhouse on Point Lobos, just south of Carmel. The family includes an aimless older brother, a broken-down, Bible-reading father, an aunt who sees visions and talks to the dead, and another aunt who has the mind of a demented child. The ghost of Tamar's mother is also present, as is the ghost of one more aunt. In that forsaken place, where the winds blow and the surf pounds and there is "never a moment of quiet," Tamar and her brother begin an incestuous relationship that eventually ends in pregnancy. What Tamar regards as an independent act of self-assertion, in which scorn for conventional morality is displayed, soon becomes something quite different. Through her aunts she learns that she is a player in a drama much larger than herself, one that involves her father, his dead sister, and their incest many years before. That "makes me nothing," Tamar says, "my darling sin a shadow and me a doll on wires." After seducing a neighbor so the paternity of the child can be concealed, and after enduring the assault of phantoms during an orgiastic seance on the shore, Tamar becomes obsessed with destruction. In the penultimate scene of the story, she has her way. Her brother stabs her lover as the house is set on fire. Everyone perishes in the conflagration that ensues. The last reference is to nature, destined to outlast the momentary passions of people.

Grass grows where the flame flowered;
A hollowed lawn strewn with a few black stones
And the brick of broken chimneys; all about there
The old trees, some of them scarred with fire, endure the sea wind.

The story Jeffers tells is extremely dense. On one level, it is a tale of gothic horror. On another, it is a study of what the strange landscape around Carmel can do to people. Early in the narrative, as Tamar undresses and joins her naked brother for a swim, Jeffers asks, "was it the wild rock coast/Of her breeding, and the reckless wind/ In the beaten trees and the gaunt booming crashes/ Of breakers under the rocks . . . taught her this freedom?" The poem is also about incest, both as a fact of life and as a symbol for human introversion. As such, it makes use of a theme found in other literary works; in the foreword to *Selected Poetry,* Jeffers mentions Shelley's *Cenci.* On another level, the poem is about World War I, for which Tamar herself serves as a symbol. And the poem refers the reader to the Bible, where the story of Tamar, daughter of David, can be found. Beneath these levels, however, and many more, there is the myth that gives the poem its power—the myth of Mother Earth.

Worship of the goddess antedates all the recorded stories told about her. As evidence from prehistoric caves suggests, she was at the center of the first known religion. Sometimes sculpted with a crescent moon or horn of plenty in her hands, she was worshipped as the source and end of life, the being on whom the cycle of the seasons depends. By the time civilization appeared, her cult was widespread, her various powers and personality traits were differentiated, and she was known by many names: Isis, Ishtar, Astarte, Asherah, Cybele, and Ge, to name a few. In some cultures, stories were told about her that involve a husband/son/brother/lover whose untimely death plunges her into such deep mourning that everything on earth stops growing. Somehow, however, she finds a way to bring her consort back to life. When he appears, earth shares in her rejoicing, a rebirth occurs, and the barrenness of winter is followed by the fecundity of spring. Or, as in the lands where many of the earliest stories were told, the season of drought is followed by the season of rain.

Tamar is modeled on this myth. The main action of the poem takes place at a time when life is moving toward an end.

> *The year went up to its annual mountain of death, gilded with*
> *hateful sunlight, waiting rain.*
> *Stagnant waters decayed, the trickling springs that all the misty-*
> *hooded summer had fed*

> *Pendulous green under the granite ocean-cliffs dried and turned*
> *foul, the rock-flowers faded,*
> *And Tamar felt in her blood the filth and fever of the season.*

Tamar herself, as this passage indicates, is attuned to the cosmic rhythm. So much so, in fact, that she becomes the means through which death is brought to the human world.

In becoming an embodiment of archetypal feminine power, she loses any trace of normal womanhood.

> *She in the starlight*
> *And little noises of the rising tide*
> *Naked and not ashamed bore a third part*
> *With the ocean and keen stars in the consistence*
> *And dignity of the world. She was white stone,*
> *Passion and despair and grief had stripped away*
> *Whatever is rounded and approachable*
> *In the body of woman, hers looked hard, long lines*
> *Narrowing down from the shoulder-bones, no appeal,*
> *A weapon and no sheath, fire without fuel . . . .*

Even so, she finds peace and joy in her identity and freedom in her destiny.

In the calm before the fire storm, when she knows for certain that she will be the torch that sets her rotten house aflame, she tells her father that time stands still. "All times are now," she says, affirming the cycle of destruction and renewal that creates permanence through change, "to-day plays on last year and the inch of our future / Made the first morning of the world."

Jeffers wrote *Tamar* in 1922, the same year that T. S. Eliot published *The Waste Land*, and it is important to note that both poets made use of the same myth in their independent efforts to describe the post-war world they were living in. Like Jeffers, Eliot locates the action of his poem in a place "where the sun beats, / And the dead tree gives no shelter, the cricket no relief, / And the dry stone no sound of water." In that desolate landscape, people with "red sullen faces sneer and snarl" at each other, engage in fruitless sexual encounters, drift into madness, or manifest any of a number of other symptoms of existential despair.

They await the burning described in the section titled "The Fire Sermon" or the drowning in "Death by Water."

As Eliot says in his footnotes, "not only the title, but the plan and a good deal of the incidental symbolism of the poem were suggested by Miss Jessie L. Weston's book on the Grail legend: *From Ritual to Romance*." In that book, Weston argues that beneath the story of Jesus that informs medieval tales about the Holy Grail, there are stories about dying and rising gods that can be traced back to the dawn of human history. "The name of the god, and certain details of the ritual, may differ in different countries," she says, "but whether he hails from Babylon, Phrygia, or Phoenicia, whether he be called Tammuz, Attis, or Adonis, the main lines of the story are fixed and invariable."

> Always he is young and beautiful, always the beloved of a great goddess; always he is the victim of a tragic and untimely death, a death which entails bitter loss and misfortune on a mourning world, and which, for the salvation of that world, is followed by a resurrection. Death and Resurrection, mourning and rejoicing, present themselves in sharp antithesis in each and all of the forms (RR 143).

Eliot adds that he also made use of Sir James Frazer's work on fertility myths found in *The Golden Bough*.

Though Eliot found the myths he needed primarily through reading, which in no way diminishes their fitness or power, Jeffers found what he was looking for primarily through an immediate experience of nature. He had read Frazer and was familiar with the ancient stories, but he did not make use of them in the self-conscious way that Eliot did. Moreover, Eliot emphasized the masculine features of the myth, those that involved the dying god, whereas Jeffers emphasized the feminine features, those that involved the Goddess behind the god.

From the writing of *Tamar* on, the Goddess was very much a part of Jeffers. Or, to put this differently, *Tamar* registers an infusion of feminine energy that forever changed his life and art.

Perhaps the death of Jeffers' mother, in March 1921, had something to do with this. As she assumed a place in the underworld of his psyche, she could have served as the matrix for the surge of feminine power that occurred. Or perhaps his experience with the "dark beauty" he met under Mal Paso Bridge a few years before released untapped anima energy within. Una certainly affected him. Her wildness offered access to modes of being and awareness not normally his own.

It was for Una, whom he thought of as a falcon, that he built Hawk Tower (at the same time *Tamar* was written). And it was for Una that he prepared a place inside the tower for a gift she had been given.

The gift was a small wax figurine of a Spanish or Indian woman with dark eyes, red lips, and long black hair pulled back from a beautiful face. The hand of her right arm is lost, as is her left arm and legs, but she wears a black velvet dress that conceals what is missing, along with a lace shoulder shawl and red cape.

The antique doll was placed in a niche in Una's room, on the second floor of the tower, in an alcove formed by oriel windows that overlook the ocean. She shares the space with other emblems of feminine power. Her back rests against a tile from the Babylonian temple of Erich that dates from about 2100 B.C., a tile that is inscribed in cuneiform with a prayer to the goddess Ishtar. She faces another niche that contains a carved stone head of an *asparas* from the Angkor temple of Prah Khan in Cambodia. *Asparases* are heavenly courtesans, or celestial dancers, once associated with primitive fertility rites. In Vedic literature they are described as spirits of water who manifest themselves in voluptuous female forms. They are known to entice men to intercourse and then to destroy them. The doll's own niche is outlined in gold paint. At one time it also contained a medal Una found in the Cathedral of Milan and a small rosary found at the base of a round tower in Kells, Ireland. There is evidence that a candle had been placed there too, for the top of the niche is blackened. Above the niche Jeffers painted an inscription: "B.V. de la torre," which stood for "Blessed Virgin of the Tower."

The Virgin Mary, Christendom's own Great Goddess, was very much a part of the place where Robinson and Una lived. When Father Junípero Serra and company performed the ceremonies that dedicated northern California to Spain, he had with him in Monterey a large wooden statue of the Virgin called "Our Lady of Bethlehem." The exquisitely carved image, still to be seen at the mission, was dressed in elegant robes and wore a golden crown. Throughout the years of Spanish colonization, the statue was highly revered, especially by sailors, and many people undertook pilgrimages to pay homage at its shrine. The Virgin was regarded as the patroness of California. That she had dominion over the land around Carmel is reflected in another name by which her statue there was known: La Conquistadora.

Whatever power was working through him, however one describes his muse—as Hawk of Shiva or Blessed Virgin—the fact remains that Jeffers created, throughout his ensuing career, some of the strongest, fiercest, most undomesticated women in modern literature. From *Tamar* to *Medea*, they leapt from his forehead like Athenas, fully armed.

Tamar and Other Poems was first printed by Jeffers at his own expense. After the release of *Californians* in 1916, he sent manuscripts to several different publishing companies but all were refused. Editors at Macmillan returned a collection of poems in 1920 because they believed it lacked the "grace and charm" of his earlier work. In 1922, Una provided Jimmy Hopper with a manuscript to take with him on a trip to New York, hoping he could interest some influential friends. One critic thought the poems were "too dirty," however, and another reader thought they were too long. Editors at Boni & Liveright flatly rejected them.

Though Jeffers liked *Tamar* and was convinced it was better than anything he had ever done, he decided not to submit it to anyone. Rather, early in 1924, he sent the manuscript to Peter G. Boyle, a printer in New York, with an order for five hundred copies. Mr. Boyle shared Jeffers' enthusiasm and tried to promote the book by sending copies to reviewers, but nothing happened. Four hundred and fifty volumes of *Tamar and Other Poems* were packed in a crate and shipped to Carmel. When they arrived, they were stored in the attic of Tor House under the eaves.

It was during this time that the Book Club of California was preparing an anthology of poems by California writers. James

Rorty, Genevieve Taggard, and George Sterling were serving as editors. Someone remembered Jeffers' work from eight years before and asked him to contribute. The poems Jeffers submitted were so impressive that one was selected for the title piece. *Continent's End: An Anthology of Contemporary California Poets* appeared in 1925.

As a token of friendship and esteem, Jeffers sent Rorty and Sterling copies of *Tamar and Other Poems*. Both were overwhelmed with what they read. Sterling shared the book with friends in San Francisco while Rorty carried it with him to New York. "*Habent sua fata libelli*"—Jeffers later said, "little books have such queer destinies" (BWJ 155).

Rorty's review, published in the book section of the *New York Herald Tribune*, March 1, 1925, reveals exactly how he felt. He describes the "extraordinary virtuosity" of Jeffers' work and then calls the title poem "a magnificent tour de force. . . . Nothing as good of its kind has been written in America." "Out of the eight-point machine-set type of the cheaply printed volume," he adds, "the great hills of the coast range rise and take their places, the brown earth cracks beneath the glare of the California sun, the 'earth-ending' waters of the Pacific heap themselves upon the lava beds. California has another great writer to place beside John Muir. America has a new poet of genius."

Rorty's review was soon followed by that of one of his friends, Mark Van Doren. Writing in the March 11 issue of *The Nation*, Van Doren chastises publishers for neglecting Jeffers and expresses his own enthusiasm.

> The most rousing volume of verse I have seen in a long time comes, it appears, from California. I am told that *Tamar and Other Poems* (New York: Peter G. Boyle), attracted no attention whatever when it was published here last summer. I did not see it then, and I am able to understand how those who did cast a glance at it failed to get very far. For the paper is coarse and the type is so small as to be painful. Yet the neglect of the book is decidedly to the discredit of New York criticism, as the necessity of its being printed at the author's expense is a disgrace to American publishing. Few recent volumes of any sort have

struck me with such force as this one has; few are as rich with the beauty and strength which belong to genius alone.

Rorty also showed *Tamar* to Babette Deutsch, whose review appeared on May 27, 1925, in *The New Republic*. The work "is hard and cool and precious as amber," she says, "and like amber, charged with electricity." "This reviewer," she adds, seeking words that could capture the excitement she experienced while reading Jeffers, "felt somewhat as Keats professed to feel, on looking into Chapman's Homer."

James Daly's review, which includes a description of a similar first encounter, appeared in the August edition of *Poetry*.

> I remember that day last summer when I opened his book. I had no especial anticipation; the work and the man were both unknown to me, the book was privately printed, the paper is coarse and the type too small. But before I had read a page my listlessness was gone, I was tense with excitement. Here was writing that seemed to spring from genius of a deep poetic compulsion, writing that had what one rarely finds in contemporary poetry—genuine passion. Here, page upon page, was a nuggeted ruggedness of imagery. Here was magnificent rhythm, responsive to the spur and rein of the thought riding it. And here were a beauty and vigor and objective immediacy of phrase—prolific, seemingly unpremeditated, yet restrained—which I dared to think unsurpassed by any other poet writing today in English.

Such praise did not go unnoticed. Demand for the book was high, but all the copies were still in Jeffers' attic. Eventually, the crate, "as big as a coffin," was hauled down and shipped back to New York, where it quickly emptied. A second edition was proposed, but Boyle, knowing he could not do justice to the book, offered it to Boni & Liveright. This time the editors there accepted. A new volume was planned that would contain everything in *Tamar and Other Poems* plus additional work.

George Sterling made the announcement in the November issue of *The Overland Monthly*. "Those of you who have not read that unforgettable poem," he says, referring to *Tamar*, "will now have their chance." He warns his readers, though, that *Tamar* is not for the faint of heart.

It is the strongest and most dreadful poem that I have ever read or heard of, a mingling of such terror and beauty that for a symbol of it I am reminded of great serpents coiled around high and translucent jars of poison, gleaming with a thousand hues of witch-fire. For Mr. Jeffers has put everything into his poem, and its huge rhythms are those of the very ocean on which his tower of granite looks forth.

Suddenly, Jeffers was famous.

It is easy to understand why Sterling liked Jeffers' work. It preserved some of the best features of the poetry Sterling admired and yet still managed to break new ground. It was, for instance, a long narrative poem written at a time when short lyrics were in vogue. In addition, it conformed to and yet transcended traditional metrical schemes, as James Daly makes clear in his analysis of *Tamar* in *Poetry*, August 1925.

> Seeing that the customary measure of blank verse moves too rapidly for the slow pulse of many of his rhythms, Mr. Jeffers thought of doubling the lines, as a lyrical trimeter was doubled to make hexameters; he then had ten bars to the line instead of five. But fearing that this measure alone would prove too heavy for the long contemporary story he wished to tell, he sought the variety of a further tidal recurrence by alternating a succession of ten-bar lines with a succession of five-bar ones. And then to ease the transitions and to satisfy his inner ear, he granted himself the Elizabethan playwright's license to leave many lines irregular; so many, in fact, that the result frequently is a thing Mr. Jeffers probably never expected to find himself writing—free verse! And it is free verse of a high order.

Sterling appreciated this kind of craftsmanship, especially since he believed that most modern poetry was being written without it. He also liked the content of *Tamar*. The story of an intensely erotic woman with destructive power appealed to his interest in *femmes fatales*. Such women were stock figures in decadent literature, as he himself had demonstrated in two recently completed verse dramas, *Lilith* and *Rosamund*. Sterling knew, however, that his own characters were the product of fantasy, even feverish dream, while Jeffers' heroine seemed to come from a deeper understanding of the real thing. And of course Sterling liked the locale of *Tamar*—his own beloved Carmel.

When Sterling left Carmel in 1914, he journeyed to New York hoping to make a bigger name for himself as a writer. Californians admired his work but the East Coast literary establishment had always ignored him. He soon discovered that he was behind the times. Poets like Carl Sandburg, Robert Frost, Amy Lowell, Hilda Doolittle, Ezra Pound, and Vachel Lindsey had started a revolution, and poets like himself were clearly on the losing side. In the March 1916 issue of *Poetry*, Harriet Monroe singled Sterling out for special scorn. His work was filled with "shameless rhetoric," she says, and "the worst excesses of the Tennysonian tradition." Sterling "never *thinks*— he *deems*; he does not *ask*, but crave; he is *fain* for this and that; he deals in *emperies* and *auguries* and *antiphons*, in *causal throes* and *lethal voids*—in many other things of tinsel and fustian, the frippery of a by-gone fashion." Monroe was moved to write these words when she discovered that Sterling's name had been carved into the triumphal arch at San Francisco's Panama-Pacific International Exposition (a fair that drew 19 million visitors between February and December 1915) alongside those of Shakespeare, Milton, Goethe, and other major poets.

Sterling did not secure a New York publisher for his work until 1923, by which time he did in fact have a national reputation as a regional writer. Prior to that success, however, his life was filled with suffering. In addition to other friends and family members who had recently died, Jack London passed away, possibly by suicide, in November 1916. Sterling's former wife, Carrie, who never stopped loving him, ended her life with poetic flair in August 1918. She carefully arranged her hair, put on a dressing gown and placed a recording of Chopin's "Funeral March" on the gramophone. Then she took a lethal dose of cyanide, lay down on her bed and, listening to the somber strains of music, joined her own procession to the grave.

Despite these tragedies, perhaps because of them, Sterling lived the life of a *bon vivant*. When he returned to San Francisco in 1918, friends provided him with a room at the prestigious Bohemian Club and took care of his basic needs. This enabled him to serve the club and the city as something like an official artist in residence.

He did his best to keep the spirit of old San Francisco alive—by rolling milk cans down Telegraph Hill, sparring with professional boxers, appearing at parties dressed in a leopard skin or toga, carrying the dragon's head in Chinatown parades, and escorting visitors on tours of the city's underground. Once, when Theodore Dreiser was in town, he and his companion and Sterling were walking through Golden Gate Park at three in the morning. Sterling stopped by a pond, stripped down, swam to the center, and returned with some water lilies for Dreiser's friend. A policeman happened on the scene and was about to arrest him but let him go as soon as he found out who he was. The newspapers carried the story in the morning, prompting Sterling to perform the same stunt several times again.

Though known for his escapades, Sterling was also known for his generosity and for his love of literature and art. He shared what little money he had with anyone who needed it, including derelicts he encountered on the street. He also published regularly, read constantly, wrote a column for the *Overland Monthly* called "Rhymes and Reactions," and served other writers, especially young or unestablished ones, as a conscientious critic and friend. When asked to help with the Book Club of California's anthology, for example, "Sterling not only read every poem that was submitted, but also reread with extra care the poems that were rejected by his coeditors" (GS 56). It was Sterling, too, who selected the title of the book, insisting it be called *Continent's End*.

By the way he talked about *Tamar* and other poems sent him, Sterling made it clear to friends that he had chosen Jeffers "for the mantle of Elijah which Bierce had entrusted to his keeping" (FA 314). He regarded him as the most important poet California had yet produced.

Hearing this from Sterling left Jeffers at a loss for words. "Your letter quite toppled me over," he wrote in response to something Sterling sent him, "like that poor city in Ohio the storm visited lately; and now after two or three days I am still trying to creep out of—not a desolation—a terrible splendor. One *can't* accept such praise—and I'm not inhuman enough to put it aside—or mean enough to be critical where you have been so generous. What can I say—except that if power comes I shall try to deserve some part of what you have written" (SL 27).

Correspondence between the poets eventually drew them together. Sterling came down to Tor House for a short visit, then for an occasional weekend, once for more than a week. He always brought books for Robinson and Una, candy, and gifts for the twins. Soon, he knew Jeffers well enough to write a brief introduction to his life and work. It was titled *Robinson Jeffers: The Man and the Artist* and was published by Boni & Liveright in 1926.

Una described Sterling in a letter to a friend as having a "lined and ascetic" face along with a "shy and sweet and sensitive" disposition. On meeting him casually, she adds, one wouldn't dream that "he was notorious for his love affairs" and that "women had died and—worse—for him" (RJN #58). In another letter, Una refers to Sterling's "resilient boyish spirit" that made him, at fifty-six, "always alert and fresh for the thousand little pleasures that most people pass unnoticing."

> When he was with us he was up and out early chopping wood, crawling over the rocks, getting abalone and cooking it for breakfast (he was proud of the abalone!), making sandwiches for our lunch when we would tramp back into the hills—or out with the boys examining tracks in the road to identify the creatures who had been about in the night—coon, skunk—Then how proud he was of his bodily fitness—making Robin and Hopper swim in the icy water beyond Pt. Lobos where everyone but himself *knew* it was too cold. Then how he would sit and discuss life and philosophy and literature.

"He was the special friend of each member of our household," Una says in drawing her letter to a close, "and we shall ever remember him with devotion" (RJN #61).

There is a reason for Una's eulogistic tone. Her letter was

written just after Sterling's death, which occurred during the night of November 16, 1926. On that night, Sterling was alone in his room on "Poor Man's Row" in the Bohemian Club. For several weeks he had been awaiting a visit from his very good friend, H. L. Mencken, in preparation for which he had collected dozens of bottles of pre-Prohibition alcohol. Years of abuse had made drinking dangerous for Sterling—he now required hospitalization after a binge—but he prided himself on his ability to show fellow writers a good time. Recent visits from Edgar Lee Masters and Sinclair Lewis had been fun for Sterling, but both resulted in tremendous pain.

When Mencken's arrival was delayed, Sterling started the party without him. By the time he finally came, Sterling was already on the other side of a drunken stupor. Consciousness had returned, but, after a slow rise to the surface, it broke on a sea of agony.

On the day of November 16, Mencken found Sterling all but unable to move. Nevertheless, Sterling promised him that he would be at the banquet planned for that evening, a banquet in Mencken's honor for which Sterling was to serve as toastmaster. The time for dinner came and went, however, and Sterling could not leave his room. After the banquet was over, Mencken went upstairs to wish his friend good night, but the lights in Sterling's room were out, the door was locked, and Mencken could not rouse him.

The next morning, knocks on the door still failed to get a response. At noon, the manager of the club opened Sterling's door with his passkey and found his twisted corpse. He had taken the cyanide he had kept in his pocket for so long.

Charred bits of paper filled the room. They were all that remained of manuscripts Sterling had burned. On one of the scraps the following words were found: "Deeper into the darkness can I peer / Than most, yet find the darkness still beyond." And on another: "I walked with phantoms that ye knew not of" (TWS 317).

Jeffers knew. As he says in a short tribute to his friend, "His life was troubled and his philosophy involved hopelessness; his face, during the two or three years since I met him, had in repose even a look of torture." But, he adds, his poetry did not dwell on despair. It served, rather, as a means through which beauty could be expressed, and thus was filled with "lyric loveliness" (BWJ 135).

Sterling was important to Jeffers, more so, perhaps, than anyone else he ever met. And Jeffers was important to Sterling. In a mysterious way, they were together when Sterling died. Jeffers recounts the experience in an essay written a year later (BWJ 145).

> One night a year ago I dreamed about the interior of an ancient church, a solid place of damp stone about which the earth had crept up, beautiful in its ruin, somewhat like the Carmel Mission before they restored it. Sterling and I were there in the stone twilight, among many worshippers, and I said though it was pleasant we mustn't stay, it was time to return out-doors. But he preferred to stay, and I returned alone, and awoke. The afternoon after that night a newspaper reporter came to tell me that Sterling had died.

Hundreds of people attended Sterling's elaborate funeral. All of San Francisco mourned. At Bigin's, his favorite restaurant, patrons bowed their heads as the orchestra played Debussy's *Prélude à l'après-midi d'un faune*.

Chapter Four

Theory of Truth

One night, soon after *Tamar* was written but before it was published, Robinson and Una entertained some visitors at Tor House. Among them were a singer and two actresses. "Before the candles were lighted," Una says in describing the evening in a letter to a friend, one of the actresses, Susan Porter, "sat down in the gray twilight in the sea-window." Speaking in a deep slow monotone, she told a story of the Irish hero Cú Chulainn, "the one where he killed his son and fought the waves." The "long white figure with half-bent head" held her audience spellbound. As Una says, it was like hearing "an old saga told by a Druidess" (RJN #57).

After that impromptu performance, Laurence Strauss stood up. He was a tenor who had come to Carmel for a concert. He entertained the guests with some "delightful old ballads and some modern French things."

Darkness had fallen. Una asked the other actress, Hedwiga Reicher, to recite "Edward, Edward," the Scottish ballad about a young man who kills his hawk, his horse, and his father, abandons his wife and children, and then curses his mother. "Much to

79

everyone's surprise she rose up and did it—a *magnificent* perfor-
mance against the front door in the candlelight. She was
magnificent and beautiful—a tragedy queen of the old school."

Robinson was deeply impressed—so impressed, in fact, that
he wrote his next major poem, a verse drama, with Reicher in
mind. In the foreword to *Selected Poetry* he describes how the
poem came to be.

> *The Tower Beyond Tragedy* was suggested to me by the imposing
> personality of a Jewish actress who was our guest for a day or
> two. She was less than successful on the stage, being too tall, and
> tragic in the old-fashioned manner; but when she stood up in our
> little room under the low ceiling and recited a tragic ballad—
> "Edward, Edward"—for a few people gathered there, the expe-
> rience made me want to build a heroic poem to match her
> formidable voice and rather colossal beauty. I thought these
> would be absurdly out of place in any contemporary story, so I
> looked back toward the feet of Aeschylus, and cast this woman
> for the part of Cassandra in my poem.

Reicher served Jeffers as a visible manifestation of the arche-
typal feminine force that was working through him at this time.
As Una said, she was "a goddess in stature and mien" (SMT 113).
The part of Cassandra was perfect for her.

In Greek mythology, Cassandra is described as a beautiful
young priestess with whom Apollo falls in love. Seeking a return
for his affection, the god gives Cassandra the gift of prophecy.
She, however, spurns Apollo and refuses to enter a liaison. The
god then adds a curse to his previous blessing—though
Cassandra will always see and speak the truth, she will never be
believed.

As a daughter of Priam and Hecuba, Cassandra is a member
of the royal house of Troy. When her brother, Paris, sails to
Sparta, where Menelaus and Helen live, she foretells the doom
that will result. Near the end of the Trojan War, she tells her
people what the enormous horse contains. Nevertheless, they
bring it into their city. After Troy is destroyed, Agamemnon
claims Cassandra as a concubine and takes her with him to his
home in Mycenae.

Jeffers' poem combines the first two plays of Aeschylus' *Oresteia* and adapts the plots to his own purposes. When King Agamemnon reaches his city, he is greeted by his wife, Clytemnestra. She welcomes him warmly and offers to prepare a bath. As soon as he slips into the water, however, she stabs him with a knife—in revenge, she says, for his sacrifice of their daughter, Iphigenia, many years before. Cassandra, of course, foresees the treachery and, after the murder, continues to forecast doom.

The role of Cassandra, as Jeffers says, was inspired by Hedwiga Reicher. In a letter to a friend, he says she also stands behind Clytemnestra. It is Clytemnestra, in fact, who commands attention throughout most of the play. She is portrayed as a powerful woman who places herself above divine and human law. When she stands before an angry, frightened crowd of people, bragging of her deed with knife in hand, she keeps the crowd from turning against her by slowly taking off her clothes. A third woman in the play, Electra, was cut by Jeffers from the same cloth. Electra is Clytemnestra's daughter. After eight years of exile, she returns to Mycenae with her brother, Orestes, in order to avenge her father's death. When Orestes hesitates to kill their mother, Electra urges him on. Eventually, the deed is done. Orestes then turns his back on his sister, who offers herself to him as a wife, and wanders into the mountains, leaving the blood-soaked human world behind.

After *The Tower Beyond Tragedy* was completed, Jeffers cast about for another story to tell. What came was a poem called *Roan Stallion*. In the foreword to *Selected Poetry,* he describes it as a narrative which "originated from an abandoned cabin that we discovered in a roadless hollow of the hills." When Robinson and Una asked about the cabin, "no one was able to tell us anything except that the place had been abandoned ever since its owner was killed by a stallion."

> This is the only one of my poems of which I can remember clearly the moment of conception. I had just finished *The Tower Beyond Tragedy* and was looking about for another subject— which was to be contemporary, because I repented of using a

Greek story when there were so many new ones at hand. I was quarrying granite under the sea-cliff to build our house with, and slacking on the job sat down on a wet rock to look at the sunset and think about my next poem. The stallion and the desolate cabin came to mind; then immediately, for persons of the drama, came the Indian woman and her white husband, real persons whom I had often seen driving through our village in a ramshackle buggy. The episode of the woman swimming her horse through a storm-swollen ford at night came also; it was part of her actual history . . . . So that when I stood up and began to handle stones again, the poem had already made itself in my mind.

The Indian woman Jeffers knew from real life became "only a fourth part Indian" in his poem. "A Scottish sailor had planted her in young native earth,/Spanish and Indian, twenty-one years before." The sailor named her "California" and then disappeared. Jeffers describes her as "a nobly formed woman" with dark, stolid features "sculptured into a strong grace."

As the poem opens, California's husband, Johnny, "an outcast Hollander; not old, but shriveled with bad living," returns to their ranch in Carmel Valley. Still drunk from the excesses of the night before, he leads a magnificent roan stallion which he won gambling. California, who is something of a religious visionary, eventually falls in love with the stallion and regards it as divine. One night, while her husband is away and their daughter Christine is sleeping, she opens the corral, leaps on the animal's back, and rides it into the hills. "Feeling between her thighs the labor of the great engine, the running muscles, the hard swiftness," she experiences a desire for union with the stallion that is both erotic and spiritual. As she rides "the savage and exultant strength of the world" she longs for interpenetration. This leads, when she dismounts on a moonlit hill and falls to the ground, to mystic delirium. She joins with the horse—not with her body, but with her soul.

The next night, when Johnny returns half drunk and wanting to make love, California escapes from him and runs for sanctuary to the center of the stallion's corral, which for her is sacred ground. The family dog follows her and begins to harry the horse. When Johnny climbs over the fence and drops into the corral, the stallion rears up and strikes him with his hooves. California's scream brings Christine from the house dragging a rifle. California takes the gun, aims carefully, and "without doubting, without hesitance," shoots the barking dog. She then lowers the rifle and watches the stallion finish her husband, who had been dragging his body toward the fence-line. "The roan thunder" struck with all its power; "hooves left nothing alive but teeth tore up the remnant." Finally, "moved by some obscure human fidelity," California raises the gun again. As "the stars fell from their places . . . in her mind," she fires three times. The haunches crumple sidewise, the forelegs stiffen, and "the beautiful strength" settles to the earth. California then turns on her little daughter "the mask of a woman / Who has killed God."

California, like Electra, Clytemnestra, and Cassandra, achieves the stature of an Amazon—a heroically proportioned woman who takes control of her fate, by violence if necessary. Thus, she too reveals the archetype at work in Jeffers' mind, the one made manifest by Hedwiga Reicher, his wife, and other women. The poem about California also bears the imprint of Miss Reicher's reading, an event that affected Jeffers throughout his life. Though here the influence could have been subliminal, it is important to note that California's father is said to have come from Scotland, the home of Miss Reicher's ballad, and the horse California kills is the same color as Edward's "reid-roan" stallion.

The Tower Beyond Tragedy and *Roan Stallion* were both included in the volume that Boni & Liveright released in 1925, which was titled *Roan Stallion, Tamar and Other Poems*. Critics who reviewed Jeffers' earlier book reiterated their praise. As Mark Van Doren says in *The Nation*, November 25, 1925, "All that was said a few months ago about Robinson Jeffers will have to be said again with greater emphasis." This new book, he adds, "not only contains those poems which, given an opportunity to strike the critical world, struck then so hard; it marches forth with several important new poems, one of which I am sure is a masterpiece." He concludes the review by saying, "Always with Mr. Jeffers, as with other major poets, humanity breaks into fire." Babette Deutsch, writing in *The New Republic*, February 10, 1926, also restates her enthusiasm. "This second volume," she says, "which includes the contents of the first, together with almost as many new pieces, confirms the reader in the belief that Robinson Jeffers ranks with the foremost American poets not only of his generation, but of all the generations that preceded him."

Critics who were new to Jeffers added to the ground swell of excitement. In the January 3, 1926, Book Review section of *The New York Times*, Percy A. Hutchison doubts whether "there is another poet writing in America today—or in England for that matter—who can, when he so desires, write in so indelible a fashion as the author of *Tamar*." "It seems," he says, "that there are in this book pages, many, many pages, which are equaled only by the very great."

Of course, not everyone was happy with Jeffers. Harriet Monroe, writing in the June 1926 edition of *Poetry*, acknowledges Jeffers' genius but criticizes his selection of themes. *Roan Stallion* was seen by her as a story about sex between a horse and a woman. "It is doubtful," she says in response, "whether even the most accomplished artistry would excuse the deliberate choice of so revolting a subject." Such comments, however, only increased the attention Jeffers received.

Readers were fascinated not just by the subject of *Roan Stallion* but by the message it contained. In one often-quoted passage, Jeffers interrupts the narrative with a personal observation.

> *Humanity is*
> *the start of the race; I say*
> *Humanity is the mould to break away from, the crust to*
> *break through, the coal to break into fire,*
> *The atom to be split.*

In making this statement, Jeffers renounced the entire Western tradition of Humanism—Classical, Renaissance, and Modern. He called his position "Inhumanism" and later explained that it involved "a shifting of emphasis from man to not-man; the rejection of human solipsism and recognition of the transhuman magnificence" (DA xxi). The fervor with which he expressed this notion gave his work a rare spiritual intensity. In fact, through a subsequent career that lasted forty years and spanned some fifteen major books, he wrote not just as a unique and powerful poet but as something more rare, especially in the twentieth century. Like Jeremiah, Dante, Blake, and others, he wrote as a prophet. Though only posterity will decide if his verse is equal to theirs, he, like they, brought forth a comprehensive vision of existence, one that was rooted in an experience of divine power, included a judgment concerning humankind, and interpreted past, present, and future in terms of the eternal.

Perhaps it was only a coincidence that Jeffers settled in a place named Carmel. If so, it is an interesting coincidence, at least insofar as the prophetic nature of his poetry is concerned.

Carmel was named by three Carmelite friars who landed in the area with Sebastían Viscaíno in 1602. The landscape reminded them of the birthplace of their order, Mt. Carmel in Palestine.

According to stories in the Bible, Carmel was a sacred mountain where a number of dramatic events occurred, perhaps the most extraordinary of which involved Elijah and a theophany of fire. As the story is told in 1 Kings 18, Elijah, regarding himself as the lone prophet of Yahweh, challenged 450 prophets of Baal to a duel, the intention of which was to prove once and for all whose deity ruled the world. The contest was simple—each side was to prepare a bull for sacrifice, lay it on an open altar made of wood, and then call upon its deity. "The god who answers with fire," says Elijah, "is God indeed." The worshippers of Baal were confident of victory, but all day long they prayed, danced, and gashed themselves and nothing happened; their summons failed. When it was Elijah's turn, he ordered the observers to douse his offering three times with water so that it would be more difficult to burn. He then asked God to show himself. Immediately, a fire from heaven came down, consumed the sacrifice, and licked up all the water. Having won back the hearts of his people by proving God's power, Elijah sentenced Baal's followers to death.

Hundreds of years later, Christian ascetics journeyed to Mt. Carmel so that they could be near the place where God answered Elijah's call. These monks eventually established a fellowship which later became the Carmelite religious order.

During the Counter-Reformation in Spain, the Carmelites were known for their passionate faith and missionary zeal. Two of the most famous members of the order were St. Teresa de Avila, whose ecstatic union with God was immortalized in a statue by Bernini, and St. Juan de la Cruz, author of such spiritual classics as *Dark Night of the Soul, Living Flame of Love*, and *Ascent of Mt. Carmel*. As the title of the latter work suggests, Carmel was more than just a place. It symbolized the arduous journey upward that the soul must make in its search for divine enlightenment.

The Carmelites who embarked on this journey could devote themselves to a life of active prayer or a life of prayerful action. They could retire, that is, to a convent or a monastery or work in the world as evangelists. The three friars who sailed with Viscaíno followed the latter route. When they landed in California, and named the region south of Monterey "Carmel," they must have felt an aura of sacredness.

Certainly when Father Junípero Serra established a mission there in 1771, he sensed the area's spiritual power. He was told by the Indians that his arrival was heralded by a flock of beautiful songbirds that suddenly swooped down from the sky. The birds had bright, multicolored plumage, unlike any they had ever seen. The Indians also told him that the large cross he set in the ground glowed in the dark. According to Serra, "the sorcerers and priest-dancers who roam through the night saw the cross, each night, going up high in the heavens—not of dark material as wood is, but resplendent with light, and beautiful to behold; and for that reason they regarded it with great respect, and made presents to it of all they had" (JS II 89).

Of the many missions that Serra founded along *El Camino Real*, the one in Carmel was his favorite. He used it as his headquarters, and when he died in 1784 he was buried there.

Long after the mission had fallen into ruin, obscuring Serra's grave, and long after the conquered Indians had disappeared, a vital trace of both remained. Jeffers could feel the afterglow of spiritual fervor at the mission, and he could feel, sometimes even see, "the ghosts of the tribe" crouching in the darkness around his home.

Tor House was situated about a mile from the mission on top of a midden, an area where Indians had camped for hundreds, perhaps thousands, of years. The dining room fireplace was set directly over the spot where ancient fires burned. When Jeffers excavated the site for the foundation of his chimney, he found the blackened bedrock five feet down.

It was a "haunted country," as Jeffers describes it in the title of a poem, made all the more intense when the Carmelites returned. In 1925 they built a convent not more than a hundred yards from Jeffers' home. It was called the Carmelite Monastery of Our Lady and St. Therese and contained a community of cloistered nuns. The community had no contact with the outside world; the convent was surrounded by a solid fence, ten feet high.

Jeffers was disturbed but also intrigued by the proximity of the women. As he says in a letter, "A Carmelite nunnery has established itself on our horizon, a bit too near, considering the look of the building, but it's quite exciting to have this austere colony of prayerful virgins for neighbor, prayer going on in hour shifts, we're told, night and day, without a moment's intermission. . . ." (SL 51).

Jeffers was just finishing Hawk Tower when construction of the convent began. As a result, a marble plaque that he had recently set into the wall of the third floor open platform probably seemed all the more appropriate to him. The plaque was carved with a quotation from the 68th Psalm: "Why leap ye, ye high hills? This is the hill which God desireth to dwell in."

It was almost as if the sacredness of the mountain in Palestine was transferred to California along with its name, and that Jeffers, like a modern Elijah, had found a God who would answer him in Carmel, infusing his sacrifice, his poetry, with fire.

But which God? Not Yahweh, the God of history, unless you

could strip away all the human characteristics attributed to him and recover a sense of his pure and wild power; nor Baal, the god of nature, unless you could expand his provenance to include all that the universe contains.

"God is a lion that comes in the night," says Jeffers in "The Double Axe."

> God is a hawk gliding among the stars—
> If all the stars and the earth, and the living flesh of the night that
>   flows in between them, and whatever else is beyond them,
> Were that one bird. He has a bloody beak and harsh talons,
>   he pounces and tears—. . .
> One fierce life. . . .

He is "terribly beautiful," he writes in *At the Birth of an Age*, trying to find images that can describe him.

> He is like a great flower of fire on a mountain in the night
>   of victory, he is like a great star that fills all the night,
> He is like the music and harmony of all the stars if all their
>   shining were harp-music. He has no righteousness,
> No mercy, no love.

According to Jeffers, the God who created the universe *is* the universe. As he says in "Monument," there is no substantial difference between one form of life and another.

> Erase the lines: I pray you not to love classifications:
> The thing is like a river, from source to sea-mouth
> One flowing life. We that have the honor and hardship of being
>   human
> Are one flesh with the beasts, and the beasts with the plants
> One streaming sap, and certainly the plants and algae and the earth
>   they spring from,
> Are one flesh with the stars. The classifications
> Are mostly a kind of memoria technica, use it but don't be fooled.
> It is all truly one life, red blood and tree-sap,
> Animal, mineral, sidereal, one stream, one organism, one God.

Individual phenomena have value, but only the whole is truly important, only the whole endures. Like flowers that live and die, people come into the world and pass away, as do nations, civilizations, species, planets, suns, galaxies, even universes. Only God remains, enduring "the sum of life's passions."

Jeffers' vision of existence, though focused for the most part on life in northern California, was informed by a sense of the cosmos as a whole.

A long narrative poem titled *Cawdor*, for instance, illustrates the perspective Jeffers attained. The poem is about a family that lives on a ranch in a canyon near Point Sur, a ranch that becomes the scene of an archetypal human drama. In a retelling of the Hippolytus/Phaedra story, the patriarch, Cawdor, marries a young woman who soon falls in love with his son. When the woman is spurned, she destroys everything around her. On the ranch there is a crippled eagle locked in a cage. It had received "the messenger/Of human love," a bullet in the wing, two years prior to the time the story begins and had been kept alive by Cawdor's daughter. Towards the end of the story, the fierce-eyed predator is shot by one of Cawdor's sons, this time to end its misery. Its body, looking "small and soft," falls to the floor of the cage, but simultaneously, its spirit breaks free and rises up. Jeffers describes the ever-widening "spirals of flight" as the hoarded energy of the eagle burns itself into "meteor freedom" and ascends higher and higher into the sky.

The scene of its captivity is soon left behind, the people are reduced to specks, the ranch where they lived (which was the world to them) disappears, the long canyon thins down to the width of a crack, and the surrounding forest shrinks to the size of a stain.

Eventually, the ocean takes on the appearance of "the great shield of the moon" and the coast-range hills gather into "one carven mountain, one modulated/Eagle's cry made stone." As the spirit of the eagle continues to climb, even the Sierras with their high peaks of snow "dwindle and smooth down." Finally, all that is seen is "the globed earth" suspended like a teardrop in the sky. Even that disappears, from the eagle's point of view, when it finds "death beyond death" in a headlong rush to the center of the sun.

Jeffers shared the eagle's perspective. His imagination was at home in the vast reaches of space where he experienced "the shining of night," the "eloquence of silence," the "beauty beyond beauty" of the darkness that contains the shining of every star ("Point Pinos and Point Lobos"). Earth, he knew, was a particle of dust spinning around a tiny sun, which was itself one of 250 billion stars in one of billions of galaxies in one of an infinite number of universes.

Jeffers believed that "a scientific basis is an essential condition" of thought. "We cannot take any philosophy seriously," he argued, "if it ignores or garbles the knowledge and view-points that determine the intellectual life" of the time (SL 254). Accordingly, he accepted the "Big Bang" theory of creation, which holds that our present universe exploded into existence some 20 billion years ago.

From the center of the explosion matter flew in all directions. The velocity was so great, in fact, that even now our solar system sails through space at tremendous speeds as it spirals within the drifting Milky Way. In doing so, it moves farther and farther away from everything else. No one knows if the universe will continue to expand, reach a point of maximum extension and stop, or go as far as it can and then contract (whereupon, after falling in on itself and becoming tremendously compressed, another explosion will occur). According to the latter concept, described as the theory of an oscillating universe, the pattern of expansion and contraction could have already occurred any number of times and could continue to occur forever.

Thus, says Jeffers in "The Great Explosion," accepting this position, the whole universe beats like a heart.

> It is expanding, the farthest nebulae
> Rush with the speed of light into empty space.
> It will contract, the immense navies of stars and galaxies, dust-
> clouds and nebulae
> Are recalled home, they crush against each other in one harbor, they
> stick in one lump

And then explode it, nothing can hold them down; there is no way
　　to express that explosion; all that exists
Roars into flame, the tortured fragments rush away from each other
　　into all the sky, new universes
Jewel the black breast of night; and far off the outer nebulae like
　　charging spearmen again
Invade emptiness.

Each beat, diastole and systole, separated by billions of years, is but a moment in the ongoing life of Jeffers' God.

The vitalizing blood of that God—whatever energy it is that spins electrons around the nucleus of an atom and planets around a sun—courses through everything that exists, uniting microcosmic with macrocosmic reality, just as the animating breath of that God inspires all that is.

Within God's body, all forms of life have individual life spans. Even stars that seem to shine forever burn out. Some suddenly burst forth with tremendous intensity before ending as cinders in the sky. Jeffers describes this phenomenon in a poem called "Nova."

That Nova was a moderate star like our good sun; it stored no
　　doubt a little more than it spent
Of heat and energy until the increasing tension came to the trigger-
　　point
Of a new chemistry; then what was already flaming found a new
　　manner of flaming ten-thousandfold
More brightly for a brief time; what was a pin-point fleck on a sen-
　　sitive plate at the great telescope's
Eye-piece now shouts down the steep night to the naked eye, a nine-
　　day super-star.

He adds, "It is likely our moderate/ Father the sun will some time put off his nature for a similar glory" at which time earth will be destroyed. Until then, however, "the sun shines wisely and warm" and within our solar system all is as it should be. On earth, "trees flutter green in the wind, girls take their clothes off/ To bathe in the cold ocean or to hunt love."

We are back on earth with Jeffers, a place which, in the context of a seemingly limitless universe, is small indeed. The main character in *Thurso's Landing* describes the planet as similar to "a stone for no reason falling in the night from a cliff in the hills, that makes a lonely/ Noise and a spark in the hollow darkness, and nobody sees and nobody cares." Though this is no doubt the case, the earth is all we have. "It is only a little planet," says Jeffers elsewhere, "But how beautiful it is" (CP III 450).

He agreed with the scientists of the day who argued that earth was once a fireball. After billions of years, the molten surface cooled down and produced a fetid atmosphere which contained "marsh-gas, ammonia, sulphured hydrogen." The sun stirred the thick air "with fierce lightnings and flagellations," says Jeffers in a late poem, out of which came "impossible molecules, amino-acids/ And flashy unstable proteins." Then life was born: "Its nitrogen from ammonia, carbon from methane,/ Water from the cloud and salts from the young seas." A "virus" flourished in and upon the warm ocean, a virus which eventually formed itself into cells which in turn combined to create new and ever more complex life systems. As millions and millions of years passed, countless marine creatures, amphibians, reptiles, plants, birds, and mammals worked their way up through the elements until finally apes appeared who one day gave birth to humankind. When this occurred, about five million years ago, earth acquired nothing more than another "sense-organ," another "nerve-ending," through which life could be expressed and experienced. "On other globes/ Throughout the universe," of course, "much greater nerve-endings" were being born. They too, like everything everywhere, enriched the consciousness and extended the reach of "the one being," the one God, "who is all that exists" (CP III 430).

God, it should be added, could choose to end his life at any time. But insofar as he chooses to live, he lives through all the forms of being that comprise him. He feels what they feel, sees what they see, thinks what they think. Accordingly, the price God pays for life is mental and physical pain. "If God is all," Jeffers reasons in a letter, "he must be suffering, since an unreckoned part of the universe is always suffering." Further, his suffering must be deliberate, it "must be self-inflicted, for he is all; there is no one outside him to inflict it" (SL 240). This difficult but provocative assertion receives treatment in a verse drama called *At the Birth of an Age*, where God speaks.

> *If I were quiet and emptied myself of pain,*
> > *breaking these bonds,*
> *Healing these wounds: without strain there is nothing.*
> > *Without pressure, without conditions, without pain,*
> *Is peace; that's nothing, not-being; the pure night, the perfect free-*
> > *dom, the black crystal. I have chosen*
> *Being; therefore wounds, bonds, limits and pain; the crowded mind*
> > *and the anguished nerves, experience and ecstasy.*
> *Whatever electron or atom or flesh or star or universe cries to me,*
> *Or endures in shut silence: it is my cry, my silence; I am the nerve, I*
> > *am the agony,*
> *I am the endurance. I torture myself*
> *To discover myself; trying with a little or extreme experiment each*
> > *nerve and fibril, all forms*
> *Of being, of life, of cold substance; all motions and netted complica-*
> > *tions of event,*
> *All poisons of desire, love, hatred, joy, partial peace, partial vision.*
> > *Discovery is deep and endless,*
> *Each moment of being is new: therefore I still refrain my burning*
> > *thirst from the crystal-black*
> *Water of an end.*

As the passage suggests, all forms of life are used by God for the purpose of self-discovery. Through differentiation God extends the possibilities of what can be. Thus, humankind is no more important than any other species of life, and the human mission, "To find and feel," is not very different from the mission of a bee as it pollinates a flower. The passage continues with a statement concerning man's place in the scheme of things.

> *. . . On earth rise and fall the ages of man, going*
> > *higher for a time; this age will give them*
> *Wings, their old dream, and unexampled extensions of mind; and*
> > *slowly break itself bloodily; one later*

Will give them to visit their neighbor planets and colonize the
evening star; their colonies die there; the waves
Of human dominion dwindle down their long twilight; another
nature of life will dominate the earth,
Feathered birds, drawing in their turn the planetary
Consciousness up to bright painful points, and accuse me of inflict-
ing what I endure. These also pass,
And new things are; and the shining pain . . . .

Of the five billion years of earth's history only the last five mil-
lion have included the presence of hominids, and most of those
years are shrouded in mystery. It wasn't until thirty-five thou-
sand years ago that people began to leave a painted record of
their fears and dreams on the walls of caves. Nearly thirty thou-
sand years passed before towns like Jericho and Çatal Hüyük
were established. Shortly thereafter civilization appeared in
Mesopotamia, Egypt, and elsewhere. In recent history, the last
twenty-five hundred years, the glory that was Greece flared up
and died down as did the grandeur that was Rome. Then the
Dark Ages, Middle Ages, Renaissance, and Enlightenment
appeared and disappeared, and the nineteenth and twentieth
centuries dawned. The Modern Age, along with the entire his-
tory of humankind, was seen by Jeffers as only a moment,
incredibly brief, in the life of the planet as a whole. And future
history, however many years it might include, will not alter this
by much. In fact, says Jeffers in "The Torch-Bearers' Race,"
mindful of geological time, "the life of mankind is like the life of
a man, a flutter from darkness to darkness/ Across the bright
hair of a fire."

Jeffers looked forward to the time when humanity would
cease to exist. Though he thought of man as one of the nobler
animals, and though he could see virtue in people, in his most
pessimistic moments he regarded earth as a star and the human
element as something which darkens it. In "De Rerum Virtute"
he refers to humanity as "a sick microbe"; in "Orca," he says, "the
breed of man/ Has been queer from the start. It looks like a
botched experiment that has run wild and ought to be stopped."

Though Jeffers' condemnation of humankind may sound offensive, it is important to note that such language is frequently found in prophetic poetry. Artists who make use of the mode often stand in judgment against the people of their time, excoriating them for behavior that falls short of an ideal. Anger and disgust, however, usually mask far deeper feelings. As Edward Weston said of Jeffers in his *Daybooks*, "Despite his writing I cannot feel him misanthropic: his is the bitterness of despair over humanity he really loves."

Nevertheless, Jeffers' criticism of humanity was sharp and his attack relentless.

Something went awry, Jeffers believed, when our most immediate ancestors, the apes, came down from the trees. Safety, but little food in a time of famine, had been found among the branches. Food, but no safety, was found upon the ground. As eons passed and adaptations occurred, humans learned to walk erect, ever alert to danger. They invented fire and flint weapons to help them in their struggle for survival. And they became "cruel and bloody-handed and quick-witted" in a world where "the great flesh-eaters,/Tiger and panther and the horrible fumbling bear and endless wolf-packs made life/A dream of death."

It was during that time of "shock and agony" that human consciousness as we know it was formed. It was then that we learned to celebrate survival and record our deeds in stories that were drenched in blood, like those concerning Achilles, Beowulf, Jesus and Judas, Jenghiz or Julius Caesar. It was then that we learned "trembling religion and blood-sacrifice." And it was then that we learned "to butcher beasts and to slaughter men/And hate the world" (CP III 433).

In a poem titled "Original Sin" Jeffers describes a primordial scene wherein a band of hominids captures a mammoth in a pit. Unable to kill the beast with sticks and stones, they fill the pit with fire and slowly roast it to death. As the blaze burns high, they watch "the long hairy trunk/Waver over the stifle trumpeting pain" and they are happy. "These are the people," says Jeffers. "This is the human dawn."

During that dawn, a wound was made in the brain that never

healed. Though we no longer see nor even feel it, it continues to hang open. Two obvious symptoms are a sense of separation from the rest of nature and a proclivity for cruelty.

Our wounded minds lead us to believe that we are more valuable to the universe than we really are. Like infants who live within closed worlds (insofar as they feel themselves to be central and of primary importance), older children and adults frequently separate themselves from others by inflating the significance of the personal or social structures to which they belong, like family, religion, country, civilization, or race. Moreover, the human species as a whole seems to be in love with itself. Like Narcissus, people find their own image reflected everywhere. As Orestes says in *The Tower Beyond Tragedy,*

> *I saw a vision of us move in the dark: all that we did or dreamed of*
> *Regarded each other, the man pursued the woman, the woman clung to the man, warriors and kings*
> *Strained at each other in the darkness, all loved or fought inward, each one of the lost people*
> *Sought the eyes of another that another should praise him; sought never his own but another's; the net of desire*
> *Had every nerve drawn to the center, so that they writhed like a full draught of fishes, all matted*
> *In the one mesh; when they look backward they see only a man standing at the beginning,*
> *Or forward, a man at the end; or if upward, men in the shining bitter sky striding and feasting,*
> *Whom you call Gods . . .*
> *It is all turned inward, all your desires incestuous . . . .*

Just as progeny of incestuous sexual relationships are often genetically defective because of the increased probability of disease, Jeffers believed our incestuous anthropocentrism leads to mental imbalance. The defect, passed on from generation to generation, keeps us within a prison of self-concern. Jeffers states his position clearly in a prose preface included in the 1977 edition of *The Double Axe.*

A man whose mental processes continually distort and prevent each other, so that his energy is devoted to introversion and the civil wars of the mind, is an insane man, and we pity him. But the human race is similarly insane. More than half its energy, and at the present civilized level nine-tenths of its energy, is devoted to self-interference, self-frustration, self-incitement, self-tickling, self-worship. The waste is enormous; we are able to commit and endure it because we are so firmly established on the planet; life is actually so easy, that it requires only a slight fraction of our common energies. The rest we discharge onto each other—in conflict and charity, love, jealousy, hatred, competition, govern- ment, vanity and cruelty, and that puerile passion the will to power—or for amusement. Certainly human relationships are necessary and desirable; but not to this extent. This is a kind of collective onanism, pathetic and ridiculous, or at noblest a tragic incest, and so I have represented it.

Incest was used by Jeffers with such dramatic intensity that he scandalized many of his readers. One parochial newspaper advised parents to keep his books out of their homes lest their children have "their souls scarred by the reading of this modern pagan giant's corruption." This is not "a matter of preventing curiosity," the paper adds, but of saving children "from a devas- tating decadence" (CE 177).

As the passages quoted above make clear, however, Jeffers used sex between brother and sister, father and daughter, and mother and son as a symbol for the demented passion we feel for each other—the more generalized attraction (with its extremes of love and hate) that keeps us locked within a human, all too human world.

We even delude ourselves with the notion that God is a cos- mic Father (or Father-Spirit-Son) who created us in his image and who thinks about us all the time. In truth, says Jeffers in "Explosion," there is "no God of love, no justicer of a little city like Dante's Florence, no anthropoid God/ Making command- ments." There is only a God "who does not care and will never cease." To believe otherwise is to fall prey to a ridiculous projec- tion of our own needs, fears, values, and misdirected dreams.

One of the most dedicated believers in Father God, says Jeffers, and one of the most tragically deceived, was a Hebrew poet named Jesus. In a play titled *Dear Judas* (which was banned, on theological grounds, from appearing in Boston), Jeffers portrays Jesus as a charismatic leader who fills people with "fear / And fascination" and mesmerizes them "like birds charmed by a serpent." He does so by intensifying and personalizing traditional Jewish wisdom at a time when people are riven with despair. "Whoever is overburdened," he says with open arms, "or hopeless, or wretched, / Or lies between the teeth of the world: let him come to me, I am able to save him."

What appears to be compassion, however, is really megalomania. "No man shall live / As if *I* had not lived," Jesus says to Judas, his closest friend. Simple control over people is not enough, he wants complete possession. And religion, he understands, is the means through which domination can occur. Religion worms "its way through the ears and eyes to the cup of the spirit, over-growing / The life in its pool with alien and stronger life, drugging the water at the well-head . . . ." Through religion he can be "a part of their being," inseparable from them forever. Though he admits "that this is tyrannous," and that "it is love run to lust," still he asserts with determination, "I will possess them."

Though Jesus is presented here as the kind of religious leader who uses the gullibility and desperation of people for his own self-aggrandizement, elsewhere he is presented as a sincere believer, even an object of pity. In *At the Birth of an Age*, for instance, Jesus is a disembodied spirit still trying to understand himself long after he has died. His message came from the heart, he says: "While I lived I saw my people beaten and deprived, therefore I imagined a world / Beyond life, out of time, righteousness triumphing." "I saw it so clearly," he adds, trying to justify his zeal, "towers of light, domes of music, / God's love the wings and the flame." He realizes, however, sadly and too late, that he was mistaken: "My dream was a fool. / My promises were a love-drunken madness."

Jeffers was fascinated by the contradictions in Jesus' personality. According to the Bible, "He is the Prince of Peace, and yet

He came 'not to bring peace but a sword;' He is gentle and loving yet He drives men with whips from the temple." A close reading of scripture reveals a mind that is "deep, powerful and beautiful; and strangely complex, not wholly integrated" (sмт 198).

In plumbing the depths of that mind, Jeffers found what he regarded as the crack through which creative power flowed. It involved Jesus' response to his own illegitimate birth. In *Dear Judas* Mary bemoans her guilt for having told her son that he had been fathered by God. She had no idea that her lie, told to hide embarrassment, would be believed. In "Theory of Truth," Jesus unravels the mystery for himself.

> *Here was a man who was born a bastard, and among the people*
> *That more than any in the world valued race-purity, chastity, the*
>   *prophetic splendors of the race of David.*
> *Oh intolerable wound, dimly perceived. Too loving to curse his*
>   *mother, desert-driven, devil-haunted,*
> *The beautiful young poet found truth in the desert, but found also*
> *Fantastic solution of hopeless anguish. The carpenter was not his*
>   *father? Because God was his father.*
> *Not a man sinning, but the pure holiness and power of God.*

Jeffers concludes this passage by saying that "His personal anguish and insane solution/Have stained an age; nearly two thousand years are one vast poem drunk with the wine of his blood."

Though Christianity has helped give Western civilization its restless, dynamic character, Jeffers believed that it has done far more harm than good. As a way of life, it increases rather than diminishes psychological disturbance, especially insofar as the bloody image of crucifixion is concerned. It separates people from the world in which they live by focusing their attention on the world to come. And it catches people in a net of self-concern. Based on a mistaken notion of love, one that encourages preoccupation with one's self and one's fellowmen, and on a mistaken belief that there is a God who cares for people (enough to appear on earth as one), Christianity deludes its followers into thinking that humans are the reason for and object of creation.

Humanism, as such, is not unique to Christianity. The Greeks and Romans also believed that man is the measure of all things. But Christianity, an Oriental religion superimposed on Western traditions, amplified the notion. In doing so, Jeffers writes in the preface to *At the Birth of an Age*, it provided "the tension that drew taut the frail arches of Gothic cathedrals" and helped create a civilization that is "the greatest, but also the most bewildered and self-contradictory, the least integrated, in some phases the most ignoble, that has ever existed."

The modern age, Jeffers believed, represents the final, fullest phase of that civilization, and perhaps its most contemptible. In America, the modern age was created by people who believed they had a manifest destiny to conquer the land. Inspired by passages in the Bible in which God says "Be the terror and dread" of everything that exists, and driven by dreams of greatness, early settlers pushed west. Without hunger, love, need, or mercy, they raped the continent and killed its native peoples. As they cleared fields, dammed rivers, laid roads, and built buildings, they carried civilization wherever they went and allowed it to spread like a fungus throughout the land.

Seeing "the beautiful places killed like rabbits" to make cities, Jeffers mourned "the hopeless prostration of the earth / Under men's hands and their minds" ("The Broken Balance"). He was especially concerned about California and his own coast's future. When Highway 1 was constructed between Carmel and Big Sur, for instance, he wrote a poem titled "The Coast-Road" in which a horseman looks down at the work from above. He shakes his fist at the bridge-builders, trucks, and power-shovels carving up the mountain and then rides on. The poem continues with Jeffers' own response.

> *I too*
> *Believe that the life of men who ride horses, herders of cattle on the*
> *mountain pasture, plowers of remote*
> *Rock-narrowed farms in poverty and freedom, is a good life.*
> *At the far end of those loops of road*
> *Is what will come and destroy it, a rich and vulgar and bewildered*
> *civilization dying at the core.*
> *A world that is feverishly preparing new wars, peculiarly vicious*

ones, and heavier tyrannies, a strangely
Missionary world, road-builder, wind-rider, educator, printer and
*   picture-maker and broad-caster,*
So eager, like an old drunken whore, pathetically eager to impose
*   the seduction of her fled charms*
On all that through ignorance or isolation might have escaped them.
*   I hope the weathered horseman up yonder*
Will die before he knows what this eager world will do to his chil-
*   dren. More tough-minded men*
Can repulse an old whore, or cynically accept her drunken kind-
*   nesses for what they are worth,*
But the innocent and credulous are soon corrupted.

The innocent and credulous, Jeffers believed, are trapped by
civilization like fish in a net. As he says in "The Purse-Seine,"

*   Lately I was looking from a night mountain-top*
On a wide city, the colored splendor, galaxies of light: how could I
*   help but recall the seine-net*
Gathering the luminous fish? I cannot tell you how beautiful the
*   city appeared, and a little terrible.*
I thought, We have geared the machines and locked all together into
*   interdependence; we have built the great cities; now*
There is no escape. We have gathered vast populations incapable of
*   free survival, insulated*
From the strong earth, each person in himself helpless, on all depen-
*   dent. The circle is closed, and the net*
Is being hauled in.

Caught as they are in a closed environment, people have little
more to do than turn upon each other—with a love that is insep-
arable from hate. All the various ideologies of the age, says
Jeffers in "The Broken Balance," such as capitalism, commu-
nism, or Christianity, draw people into contact and conflict with
each other. "Having no center / But in the eyes and mouths that
surround them" and "no function but to serve and support /
Civilization," it is no wonder that people "live insanely"—desir-
ing "with their tongues, progress; with their eyes, pleasure; with
their hearts, death."

And in the twentieth century, death is easily found. World Wars I and II were orgies of destruction and convulsive spasms of cruelty, vividly described by Jeffers in "The King of Beasts."

> Cattle in the slaughter-pens, laboratory dogs slowly tortured to
>   death, flogged horses, trapped fur-bearers,
> Agonies in the snow, splintering your needle teeth on chill steel—
>   look:
> Mankind, your Satans, are not very happy either. I wish you had
>   seen the battle-squalor, the bombings,
> The screaming fire-deaths. I wish you could watch the endless
>   hunger, the cold, the moaning, the hopelessness.
> I wish you could smell the Russian and the German torture-camps.
>   It is quite natural the two-footed beast
> That inflicts terror, the cage, enslavement, torment and death on all
>   other animals
> Should eat the dough that he mixes and drink the death-cup.

To Jeffers, the world wars appeared to be the very focus and violent peak of all human effort. He also knew, however, that on a smaller scale, similar tragedies had happened many times before. As he says in "Prescription of Painful Ends,"

> Lucretius felt the change of the world in his time, the great republic
>   riding to the height
> Whence every road leads downward; Plato in his time watched
>   Athens
> Dance the down path. The future is a misted landscape, no man sees
>   clearly, but at cyclic turns
> There is a change felt in the rhythm of events, as when an exhausted
>   horse
> Falters and recovers, then the rhythm of the running hoof-beats is
>   changed: he will run miles yet,
> But he must fall: we have felt it again in our own life-time, slip,
>   shift and speed-up
> In the gallop of the world; and now perceive that, come peace or
>   war, the progress of Europe and America
> Becomes a long process of deterioration—starred with famous
>   Byzantiums and Alexandrias,
> Surely,—but downward.

"I would burn my right hand in a slow fire/ To change the future," says Jeffers in "Rearmament," but to what purpose? Watching "the dance of the/ Dream-led masses down the dark mountain," the only legitimate response is awe.

One might also feel a measure of thankfulness. When civilization is destroyed, and with it most of humankind, the earth will begin to heal itself of its sickness. As Jeffers says in "Summer Holiday," buildings will collapse, roads will break apart, and wilderness will return.

> The towered-up cities
> Will be stains of rust on mounds of plaster.
> Roots will not pierce the heaps for a time, kind rains will cure them,
> Then nothing will remain of the iron age
> And all these people but a thigh-bone or so, a poem
> Stuck in the world's thought, splinters of glass
> In the rubbish dumps, a concrete dam far off in the mountain . . .

A few survivors will remain, but eventually, even this small remnant will disappear. When this occurs, says Jeffers in "Hooded Night," the world will resume its ancient splendor.

> Before the first man
> Here were the stones, the ocean, the cypresses,
> And the pallid region in the stone-rough dome of fog where the moon
> Falls on the west. Here is reality.
> The other is a spectral episode; after the inquisitive animal's
> Amusements are quiet: the dark glory.

Though earth will flourish long after humankind is gone, it is important to remember that the planet, too, will someday die. Of the many fates that could befall it Jeffers says in "Nova," one of the most likely is incineration. When our sun flares up, earth will be swallowed in flame. The "tall/ Green trees" will "become a moment's torches and vanish," the oceans will "explode into invisible steam." The "Hollows of the Pacific sea-bed might smoke for a moment," but after a time, earth will cool down. Then it will be "like the pale proud moon,/ Nothing but vitrified sand and rock."

This will not happen for quite some time, however. Meanwhile, what can people do? Given the way the world is, what makes a life worth living? Or, as Jeffers himself asks in "The Answer," what *is* the answer?

> *—Not to be deluded by dreams.*
> *To know that great civilizations have broken down into violence,*
> *and their tyrants come, many times before.*
> *When open violence appears, to avoid it with honor or choose the*
> *least ugly faction; these evils are essential.*
> *To keep one's own integrity, be merciful and uncorrupted and not*
> *wish for evil; and not be duped*
> *By dreams of universal justice or happiness. These dreams will not*
> *be fulfilled.*
> *To know this, and know that however ugly the parts appear the*
> *whole remains beautiful. A severed hand*
> *Is an ugly thing, and man disservered from the earth and stars and*
> *his history . . . for contemplation or in fact . . .*
> *Often appears atrociously ugly. Integrity is wholeness, the greatest*
> *beauty is*
> *Organic wholeness, the wholeness of life and things, the divine*
> *beauty of the universe. Love that, not man*
> *Apart from that, or else you will share man's pitiful confusions, or*
> *drown in despair when his days darken.*

In order to keep one's own integrity, recover mental health, appreciate the beauty of nature, and find a measure of truth, a person must overcome self-centeredness. In "Sign-Post" Jeffers gives the following advice.

> *Civilized, crying how to be human again: this will tell you how.*
> *Turn outward, love things, not men, turn right away from humanity.*
> *Let that doll lie. Consider if you like how the lilies grow,*
> *Lean on the silent rock until you feel its divinity*
> *Make your veins cold, look at the silent stars, let your eyes*
> *Climb the great ladder out of the pit of yourself and man.*
> *Things are so beautiful, your love will follow your eyes;*
> *Things are the God, you will love God, and not in vain,*
> *For what we love, we grow to it, we share its nature.*

Only when we turn outward can we appreciate the organic wholeness of the universe, the transhuman magnificence of life. And only then can we take our place in the stream of things.

In a letter to Sister Mary James Power, author of *Poets at Prayer*, Jeffers offers a succinct summary of the beliefs that forever guided both his life and art (SL 221).

> As to my 'religious attitudes'—you know it is a sort of tradition in this country not to talk about religion for fear of offending—I am still a little subject to the tradition, and rather dislike stating my 'attitudes' except in the course of a poem. However, they are simple. I believe that the universe is one being, all its parts are different expressions of the same energy, and they are all in communication with each other, influencing each other, therefore parts of one organic whole. (This is physics, I believe, as well as religion.) The parts change and pass, or die, people and races and rocks and stars; none of them seems to me important in itself, but only the whole. This whole is in all its parts so beautiful, and is felt by me to be so intensely in earnest, that I am compelled to love it, and to think of it as divine. It seems to me that this whole alone is worthy of the deeper sort of love; and that there is peace, freedom, I might say a kind of salvation, in turning one's affections outward toward this one God, rather than inward on one's self, or on humanity, or on human imagination and abstractions—the world of spirits.
>
> I think it is our privilege and felicity to love God for his beauty, without claiming or expecting love from him. We are not important to him, but he to us.
>
> I think that one may contribute (ever so slightly) to the beauty of things by making one's own life and environment beautiful, so far as one's power reaches. This includes moral beauty, one of the qualities of humanity, though it seems not to appear elsewhere in the universe. But I would have each person realize that his contribution is not important, its success not really a matter for exultation nor its failure for mourning; the beauty of things is sufficient without him.
>
> (An office of tragic poetry is to show that there is beauty in pain and failure as much as in success and happiness.)

Division Knoll & Bixby, Sur Coast, 1982 *(Morley Baer)*

Jeffers and George Sterling, c. 1926

Carmel Mission, 1884

Donnan, Una, Garth, and Robinson, 1924

Tor House and Hawk Tower with Jeffers and sons on turret, c. 1927

TIME

The Weekly Newsmagazine

ROBINSON JEFFERS

Volume XIX   Number 14

Front cover, *Time,* 4 April 1932

Mabel Dodge Luhan's ranch house—Taos, New Mexico, c. 1933

Mabel Dodge Luhan,
c. 1930

Robinson, Garth, Una, and Donnan—Taos, New Mexico, 1938

Jeffers, c. 1939

Una, c. 1940

Jeffers, c. 1955

Jeffers, 1956 *(Leigh Wiener)*

Chapter Five

Now Returned Home

As Jeffers' ideas took hold and his fame increased, life became a nightmare of telegrams and letters, interviews, photograph sessions, portrait painting sittings, and all the other activities that come with being a celebrity. To minimize distractions, the Jefferses hung a sign on their front gate. On one side it said "NOT AT HOME BEFORE 4 P.M.," and on the other, "NOT AT HOME." Even so, their closest friends were welcome anytime.

Among those friends, Teddie Kuster could be numbered. Una's first husband followed her to Carmel, bought adjoining property and, after Tor House was built, constructed a larger stone home about 200 yards away. This enabled him to remain in Una's life as part of her family. Garth and Donnan knew him as "Uncle Teddie." He built a theater in Carmel called The Golden Bough, which included a courtyard filled with shops, and thus became an important part of the community.

Other men felt a similar attraction to Una. There was never a time, in fact, when male friends were not an important part of her life. The same could be said for women, with whom Una established relationships that were deep and long-lasting.

The record of one extraordinary friendship is contained in a book titled *Of Una Jeffers* written by Edith Greenan, Teddie Kuster's second wife. "Everyone is richer for knowing her," Edith says therein, "and everyone who has been touched by her warm hand has been moulded by it." The depth of her affection can be measured by the fact that, after she too divorced Teddie and married again, she named her first child Maeve in honor of the daughter Una lost.

These kinds of feelings did not surprise Jeffers. In the foreword to Edith's book, he refers to "the undeserved good fortune that has followed me like a hound, ever since I knew the woman whom Edith Greenan too seems to use for pole-star."

Una certainly centered Jeffers. And she did all she could to keep their life, their cherished life at Tor House, normal. As always, she awoke in the morning and immediately took a cold bath, roaring like a lioness as she did so. Then she slipped on a simple dress, braided her hair, and prepared breakfast for the family. After breakfast, when Jeffers went upstairs to write (sometimes at her urging, for he liked to linger), Una took care of household chores.

Her children, along with Robinson, were at the center of her life. "They are stunning to look at," she says in a letter to a friend, "my gracious! how I adore them" (RJN #56). Garth was the larger of the two and, by twenty minutes, the younger. He was a strong and sturdy child with a fair complexion. Donnan had a slighter build and darker features.

The twins started school when they were eight. Prior to that time, Una taught them how to read and write. She also gave instruction in other subjects, including Latin. In this, her temper sometimes flared. Once, when she was angry at her sons, she threw their Latin book across the room.

Nothing happening in the house disturbed Jeffers. All morning long he could be heard tapping out the rhythm of his words or pacing to and fro. The smell of pipe smoke drifted down. On a good day, between thirty and fifty lines would be composed, but always at a price. Jeffers came downstairs at one o'clock in something of a daze. He looked "thinner and more gaunt" after writing; there was "a wan-ness over his cheeks and the deep clefts in the rocky face" looked deeper (UR 9).

Gradually, however, Jeffers returned to ordinary reality. He was helped in this by the meal Una served, the biggest of the day. It usually included something hearty, like pot roast, roast leg of lamb, round steak, or sole.

After lunch, Jeffers continued to work outside on the house or grounds. So did Una. She took care of the courtyard, which was covered with wild grass, wild flowers, and a carpet of sweet alyssum. To these she added bushes of rose geraniums, wallflowers, marigolds, yellow roses, irises, asphodels, liontail, gray santolina, campion, penny-royal, bergamot, lemon verbena, mint, thyme, rosemary, lavender, and a variety of other flowers and herbs. Two Irish yew trees also stood within the courtyard walls.

Not every day was spent working. On many afternoons, the family took long hikes into the surrounding hills. These were called "pilgrimages" by Una, who usually planned them. Additional spare time was used for writing letters or reading books.

In the evening, after a light supper and the customary walk along the beach, the family still sat together by the fire. As Robinson read aloud, Una unbraided her hair and slowly brushed it. The mood established by the reading stayed with everyone for a long time. "For the last three months," Una writes in a letter, "we have been reading Hardy's novels." Jeffers started with *The Mayor of Casterbridge* and continued through them all. "We are now finishing the sixth one, *Far from the Madding Crowd*," Una adds, "and have gradually built up a Wessex atmosphere and group of people—and familiar scenery that is as vivid in our minds as Tor House itself" (RJN #58).

Sometimes Una read. Edith Greenan recalls a time when she was sitting with the family by the fire "listening to the high wind which sounded like sea waves through the trees close against the house." Robinson asked Una to read John Synge's *Riders to the Sea*. "Her low voice rising and falling brought into the room the beat of the sea and the relentless surge of grief; tears streamed from her eyes" as she read the final lines (UJ 25).

Synge was a special favorite of Una's, but then anyone or anything Irish interested her. Her favorite poet was W. B. Yeats, about whom she lectured on occasion. She also studied Irish music and acquired a library of several thousand songs, many of which she played on her three reed organs or her piano. And she knew as much as anyone about Irish round towers.

Like the aroma of orange wine kept brewing on the stove, Una's interests and passions infused the house. They also breathed through her correspondence, wherein even the simplest experiences were described with intensity of emotion. "I wish you could be at Tor House today," she writes in a letter to a friend (RJN #49). "An hour ago I went outside on some small errand and have stood with beating heart leaning against the wall looking, looking—the colors my dear and the fragrance and the susurrus of the grass—the wild oat grass that covers the moor, the still little heads bow and sway in the wind with that little whisper!" In another letter, finished before going to bed, Una offers an understated yet compelling description of the weather (RJN #51).

> I have looked out our sea window. It is midnight. The sky is mostly covered with black clouds. A few pale stars in the rifts. The moon, very yellow even through its veil, is an hour from setting & its path is broad & yellow & broken & flashing from our shore to the horizon. The water pounds against our cliffs. There will be another storm before morning.

For Jeffers, the storm came with the publication of the book that followed *Roan Stallion, Tamar and Other Poems*. When *The Women at Point Sur* appeared in the summer of 1927, it was denounced by even his most ardent admirers.

The novel-length poem tells the story of the Rev. Dr. Arthur Barclay, a minister who experiences a crisis of faith just after World War I. Before embarking on a search for truth, he addresses his congregation one last time. "Christianity is false," he tells his people. "The fable that Christ was the son of God and died to save you, died and lived again. Lies." Barclay wanders southward down the coast of California until he reaches Point Sur, where he takes a room in an isolated farmhouse. In that sanctuary, a new theology takes shape in his mind, one based on the notion that "God thinks through action." There is no difference between right and wrong, Barclay concludes, and, with that as his message, he becomes the prophet of a new religion.

Barclay shares his message with the troubled manager of the ranch, Natalia Morhead. Natalia's husband, Randall, left her and his father in charge of things when he went off to fight in the war. "Old Morhead," however, had an accident soon after his son departed and lies paralyzed in an upstairs room. He is cared for by Faith Heriot, Natalia's bisexual lover.

Barclay shares his ideas with Faith as well and with anyone else who will listen to him. This eventually includes servants and ranch hands on the property along with people from the surrounding area. He tells his followers that God no longer cares for his old commandments and that "he is wild to walk in new ways." There is "nothing wicked" now, he says, "no sin, no wrong, no possible fountain of shame." "*Be* your desires," he advises, "break custom, flame, flame/ Enter freedom."

Barclay himself pays a Mexican serving girl to have sex with him. But this act only prepares the way for a more horrific transgression. When his daughter, April, finds him at the Morhead ranch and tries to persuade him to come home, he rapes her. April's mind breaks down over this and she begins to see herself as her brother Edward, recently killed in the war. The spectre of Edward haunts Barclay as well. Both father and daughter, in fact, think of him in terms of images drawn from the Scottish ballad. He appears to them with a sword blade in his hand, all drenched in blood.

As this is happening, Natalia's husband, Randall, returns home. His appearance heightens tension in the house because, unknown to Natalia, Randall and Faith had been lovers just before he joined the service.

Subsequent turns of the plot are impossible to summarize. Suffice it to say that several characters are sucked into a whirlpool that includes madness, murder, and suicide.

Critics, expecting more from Jeffers or something different, were disappointed by the book. They could see flashes of genius within it but, as a whole, they found it difficult to read. "For all the metaphysical meat of its content," says Babette Deutsch in the August 17, 1927, issue of *The New Republic*, "for all the lightning-like visions which streak certain passages with a glory, the poem leaves one with the feeling of having witnessed a Pyrrhic victory. Its profundities are too often obscure. Its drama is moiled with an irrelevant sordidness. There are too many persons, too many conflicts, that seem to have no organic relation to the whole. It is not sufficiently stripped and bare." "Perhaps the critics turned Mr. Jeffers' head," says Percy Hutchison in the September 11, 1927, Book Review section of the *New York Times*. "And perhaps, which would be sad indeed, his poetic genius is spent and the white flame is no longer at his command." "I may be brought to wonder," says Mark Van Doren in the July 27, 1927, issue of *The Nation*, after finding the book thrilling but "unbearable" to read, "whether there is need of his trying further in this direction. He seems to be knocking his head to pieces against the night."

Genevieve Taggard, one of the first discoverers of Jeffers, was less kind. Writing in the August 28, 1927, Book Section of the *New York Herald-Tribune*, she refers to "the terrific death" that Jeffers seemed to be experiencing. "His work has failed," she says, and "in its stupendous wreckage," it "suggests something that might have been supreme." *The Women at Point Sur* is filled with nonsense, Taggard argues, and represents little more than "a ridiculous, belated second flowering" of ideas suggested by Nietzsche. "Hardly anyone living could succeed in writing as badly." "The world is probably not as sick as Jeffers feels it to be," she concludes. "If it were sick enough to accept Jeffers, it could hardly live long enough to do so."

Despite such criticism, Jeffers stood behind his poem. Before it was published he referred to it in a letter to his editor, with an uncharacteristic expression of pride, as "the Faust of this generation" (SL 105). After it appeared, he defended it by saying it was worth several *Tamars*. He acknowledged problems with the poem, saying in a letter to a friend that its density requires a reader "to hold too many things in mind at once" (SL 117), but he remained confident that someday it would be understood.

At any rate, the adverse response in no way slowed his career. By 1928 Jeffers was well known in both Europe and America. Leonard and Virginia Woolf published *Roan Stallion, Tamar and Other Poems* at their Hogarth Press in London during that year, and an excerpt from *Roan Stallion,* translated into French, appeared in a Paris volume titled *Anthologie de la Nouvelle Poésie Américaine.* Also in 1928, the Book Club of California printed a small selection of Jeffers' work, and Liveright published his next major book, *Cawdor and Other Poems. Dear Judas* appeared in London the following year. In 1931 *Descent to the Dead* came out and, in 1932, *Thurso's Landing and Other Poems.*

Throughout this fruitful period, critical response continued to be mixed. It covered the entire spectrum—from unrestrained enthusiasm to vitriolic condemnation. Anne Singleton spoke for those who cared deeply for Jeffers in a review of *Cawdor* published December 23, 1928, in the *New York Herald-Tribune.* Referring to the failure of tragedy to induce catharsis in modern readers, she says that Jeffers' work uncovers the genre's ancient power: "From first to last Robinson Jeffers turns up with his verse the fresh earth of experienced tragedy, the stuff of reality that 'Oedipus Rex' must have had in it when the material it was made of was still alive and compelling in men's minds." "It seems to me," she says, that "Robinson Jeffers is writing the most powerful, the most challenging poetry of this generation." In addition to the startling effect produced by his long narratives, his short lyrics "focus in small compass the incredible strength and sureness of the poet and reach an intensity not touched elsewhere in modern verse."

In his *In Defense of Reason,* Yvor Winters spoke for those who detested Jeffers when he called his writing "pretentious trash" filled with little more than doctrinaire "hysteria." "There is an endless, violent monotony of movement" in Jeffers' verse, he says in the summer 1932 issue of *Hound & Horn,* "wholly uninteresting and insensitive, that may have a hypnotic effect upon a good many readers, much as does the jolting of a railroad coach over a bad roadbed." His writing is "loose, turgid, and careless," he argues in the February, 1930, issue of *Poetry.* "One might classify

Mr. Jeffers as a 'great failure' if one meant by the phrase that he had wasted unusual talents; but not if one meant that he had failed in a major effort, for his aims are badly thought-out and are essentially trivial."

The middle way was expressed by critics like Mark Van Doren and Louis Untermeyer. Despite some very real concerns about the content of Jeffers' poems and the effectiveness of his rhythms, which sometimes seemed to sound like prose, Van Doren says that "Mr. Jeffers should not be tampered with." There is no sense in defending or attacking him, he argues in *The Nation*, January 9, 1929. "The vehicle of his verse was slowly and painfully built, and it may be left alone in its power. It will outride any storm." Untermeyer says something similar in *The Yale Review*, June 1932. Though the philosophy expressed by Jeffers may be "negative, repetitious," and "dismal," it must be experienced and endured. Whether one likes or dislikes Jeffers is thus irrelevant.

> The poetry, even when bitterest, is positive as any creative expression must be; it is varied in movement and color, it vibrates with a reckless fecundity. It is like nothing else of which we are proud to boast; it is continually breaking through its own pattern to dangerous and unfathomed depths. This is not a work to be enjoyed without sacrificing that sense of ease dear to the casual reader; I am not sure that, in the common sense, it can be 'enjoyed' at all. But here is an undeviating, full-throated poetry, remarkable in sheer drive and harrowing drama, a poetry we may never love but one we cannot forget.

Whatever one thought of him, there was no denying his fame. In April 1932, a picture of Jeffers standing with his two sons in the door to Hawk Tower was published in *Vanity Fair*. The accompanying article begins with the statement, "In the eyes of many, Robinson Jeffers is America's greatest poet." In the same month he was featured on the cover of *Time*.

Jeffers' success as a poet enabled him to survive the collapse of his publisher, Horace Liveright. When the firm declared bankruptcy in 1932, other publishers went after the few important authors it had left. "Everybody was making offers for Eugene O'Neill," says Bennett Cerf, one of the founders of Random House, "and also for one of the leading American poets who was on the Liveright list, Robinson Jeffers." Jeffers "had become a topic of conversation because of his passionate poetry," he adds, and "there was great prestige in publishing him." Thirteen companies approached Jeffers, but it was Cerf's offer from Random House, delivered in person, that carried the day. Accordingly, Random House reissued five of Jeffers' previous books in 1933 and released a new work titled *Give Your Heart to the Hawks*. The firm also announced that it would be Jeffers' exclusive publisher in America from that time on.

When Cerf visited them at Tor House, Robinson and Una no doubt entertained him much as they did any of their other interesting, important, or distinguished guests: with cordial conversation and a glass of home-made wine. Both, by now, were being offered to an ever-widening circle of acquaintances and friends. Among the poets and writers included in that circle were Edgar Lee Masters, Carl Sandburg, Sara Bard Field, Charles Erskine Scott Wood, Edna St. Vincent Millay, Langston Hughes, Dorothy Parker, George Russell, Sinclair Lewis, Arthur Davison Ficke, Irvin S. Cobb, William Rose Benét, William Saroyan, Aldous Huxley, Lincoln Steffens, Thornton Wilder, Jean Toomer, and Martin Flavin. Artists and intellectuals from other fields were included too, like George Gershwin, Leopold Stowkowski, Charlie Chaplin, James Cagney, Roland Young, Martha Graham, Charles Lindbergh, Krishnamurti, Ansel Adams, Edward Weston, and Ella Winter. Add to this list the not so famous friends who liked to drop by, the friends of friends vacationing in Carmel, the loyal or angry readers who wanted to meet Jeffers, and the people with business at his home, and it is easy to understand why Robinson and Una needed a sign on their front gate.

But this did not always work. Three college students appeared at Tor House in the middle of a storm one night and insisted on talking with Jeffers about the meaning of life. They stayed well into the early hours of the morning. On another rainy night, Robinson and Una were sitting by the fire with a friend when they heard a knock on the door. Jeffers opened it to a man who said simply, "Are you Mr. Jeffers?" When Jeffers said "Yes," the man added "Come with me." Jeffers threw a rain cape over his shoulders and disappeared into the darkness. He returned a few minutes later with a smile on his face. The stranger turned out to be a chauffeur who led Jeffers to a car parked in the road. A bejewelled dowager sat inside. "Oh, so you are Robinson Jeffers," she said as the chauffeur opened the door. "I just wanted to see what you look like." Una was furious. "Where is my shotgun?" she exclaimed before she calmed down and started laughing, "I will shoot that woman" (RJN #53). According to Langston Hughes, this was no idle threat. When he came to Carmel, friends told him that Una "once fired point-blank at some curious tourists who climbed over the rocks to the very windows of Tor House" (RJN #55).

Una might well have guarded herself and her husband more carefully from the attention of one wealthy woman, with an attitude similar to that of the lady in the limousine, who worked her way into the Jeffers home and subsequently had a profound effect upon it. But then, few people could stand up against Mabel Dodge Luhan.

As Lois Rudnick, her biographer, tells the story, Luhan was born into a wealthy family from Buffalo. After her first husband was killed in a hunting accident, she moved with her second husband to Florence, Italy. In 1905, she purchased and renovated a villa built by the Medici family during the Renaissance. She lived there as if she *were* a Medici, even dressing to fit the part. She filled her home with interesting people and beautiful *objets d'art*. Gertrude and Leo Stein were among her friends during this period, as were André Gide, Bernard Berenson, and Arthur Rubinstein.

While keeping her villa for future use, Mabel left Italy in 1912 and moved to New York. Soon after, she separated from her husband. For the next few years, her apartment on Washington Square in Greenwich Village served the city as one of its most important meeting places for artists and intellectuals. "Movers and shakers," as Mabel herself called them, could be found there almost anytime and certainly on Wednesday or Thursday evenings, when Mabel hosted an open debate followed by a lavish buffet at midnight. A. A. Brill, Emma Goldman, Walter Lippmann, Lincoln Steffens, Max Eastman, Margaret Sanger, Alfred Stieglitz, Isadora Duncan, and John Reed were drawn to Mabel's salon, where the spirit of revolution was always in the air. John Reed, author of *Ten Days That Shook the World*, fell in love with Mabel and asked her to marry him.

Mabel had other plans, however. In 1917, she moved with her third husband, Maurice Sterne, to Taos, New Mexico. She found there a place of pristine beauty that made a deep impression on her. When she encountered the Pueblo Indians who lived nearby she felt she had discovered a wellspring of ancient wisdom, wisdom that could be used to revitalize an otherwise dying Western civilization. Her feelings were confirmed by an occultist who told her about a cosmic plan in which Mabel had been selected to serve as a bridge between the white and Indian worlds.

In seeking to fulfill her vocation, Mabel divorced Sterne and married a full-blooded Tiwa, Antonio Luhan. Soon thereafter, she purchased land near Taos and built an estate that included five guest cottages in addition to her own seventeen-room home. She then began inviting "great souls" to join her at Taos, hoping they would experience the power of the place and express it through their art, music, or writing. Mary Austin, Willa Cather, Edna Ferber, Thornton Wilder, Thomas Wolfe, Georgia O'Keeffe, and Ansel Adams answered her call. So did D. H. Lawrence, who Mabel hoped would serve as her preeminent prophet.

Mabel drew Lawrence to Taos by supplementing her letters to him with Indian magic and nightly transmissions of energy from her solar plexus. The spell did not last long, however, because Lawrence saw through Mabel soon after he arrived. In a letter to his wife's mother, he describes Mabel as "a little famous in New York and little loved, very intelligent as a woman, a 'culture carrier,' likes to play the patroness, hates the white world and loves the Indian out of hate, is very 'generous,' wants to be 'good' and is very wicked, has a terrible will-to-power, you know—she wants to be a witch and at the same time a Mary of Bethany at Jesus's feet—a big white crow, a cooing raven of ill omen, a white buffalo" (PL 354). Nevertheless, Lawrence lived on or near Mabel's property for about three years. He returned to England in 1925, leaving Mabel with a feeling of failure. Lawrence wrote prolifically during this period, producing such works as *The Woman Who Rode Away, St. Mawr*, and *The Plumed Serpent*, but he never gave Taos the voice Mabel was hoping for.

In trying to make the best of the situation, Mabel imagined that Lawrence served as a John the Baptist. She believed that he had prepared a way in the wilderness for a prophet yet to come. When Mabel met Jeffers early in 1930, she was convinced she had found her man.

Robinson and Una had just returned from a long vacation in the British Isles. From June to December in 1929 they traveled with their sons through Ireland, Scotland, and England. Friends who welcomed them home introduced them to Mabel. She was in Carmel for the winter, hard at work on her memoirs. Una, like Frieda Lawrence before her, enjoyed Mabel's company and soon became her friend.

Believing that Lawrence and Jeffers would benefit from knowing each other, Mabel secured two autographed books from Jeffers and sent them abroad. Lawrence died, however, before receiving them. In response to this, Mabel abandoned her autobiography and began work on a different kind of project: a book-length letter to Jeffers about Lawrence's sojourn in the American Southwest. Through March and April 1930, Mabel shared her work with Robinson and Una on an almost daily basis. By May she had convinced them that they and their children should come to Taos to see for themselves what she was writing about. June found the family there, somewhat puzzled as to how and why.

Mabel's ulterior motive surfaced later. Near the end of her letter to Jeffers, which was published as *Lorenzo in Taos* in 1932, she states it clearly.

Well, Jeffers, that is all I have to tell you about Lawrence in Taos.

I called him there, but he did not do what I called him to do. He did another thing. Perhaps you are the one who will, after all, do what I wanted him to do: give a voice to this speechless land. Something interfered with Lorenzo's chance to do that. Perhaps it was because there was too much willfulness and passion and egotism surrounding him here. The irony of it is that if there is a greater freedom and purity in my wish now, that the life here may become articulate, and that you will be the channel through which it shall speak, it is Lorenzo who released me from my insistent self-will and brought me to the happy immolation that has in it no false desire. You are a clear channel and I think I am become myself a clear one, now, too.

Whatever Jeffers might have been, Mabel was anything but a clear channel, as events in Taos subsequently revealed.

After their first visit in 1930, the Jefferses did not return until the summer of 1933. Thereafter, they visited in 1934, 1935, 1936, 1937 (on the way back from another six-month trip to the British Isles), and 1938. For all the time he spent there, four to six weeks on each occasion, Jeffers wrote only one short poem about Taos. This left Mabel feeling like a failure once again.

In 1938, she got her revenge.

Robinson was emotionally drained when he arrived in Taos that year. Throughout the decade, despite success, he had suffered from bouts of severe depression. These were caused by many factors, including distress over the ever-increasing popularity of Carmel. Tourists who flocked to the area liked to picnic on the rocks below Tor House. Jeffers erected signs that said "CLOSED TO MOTORISTS. NO TRESPASSING BY PERSONS LEAVING CARS ON OR NEAR THESE PROPERTY LINES" and "NO CAMPING. NO SHOOTING. DO NOT LEAVE PAPERS OR OTHER FILTH," but these did little to discourage them. Accordingly, Jeffers thought about moving. Una wrote to a friend that Jeffers had said to her, "Why *try* to stay here, there are so many wild places left." For her part, Una did all she could "to give Robin an illusion of a wilder, more rural home." "Life has been going smoothly here," she says in another letter, with "me sitting on the lid! We have gone off for one whole day by ourselves in the hills every week and walked for two hours late afternoons almost every day and Robin has been content" (RJN #44).

But only on a superficial level. In addition to the disgust he felt for tourists and the distress he experienced when sunny days dispelled the fog he loved so well, deeper matters disturbed him. As Jeffers grew older, he found it more and more difficult to write and he found fewer people to write for.

After *Give Your Heart to the Hawks*, which appeared in 1933, Jeffers published *Solstice* in 1935. A comment made in the preface to the opening poem states the whole book's theme: "I believe that we live about the summit of the wave of this age, and hence can see it more objectively, looking down toward the troughs on both sides." The prospect of a long slide into oblivion was not attractive to readers whose hold on life had already slipped as a result of the great Depression.

In 1937, Jeffers returned to "Edward, Edward" for inspiration. The title of the book he published that year, *Such Counsels You Gave to Me*, was taken from the ballad. The theme was long familiar—incest, madness, and murder. *Time* magazine, formerly a champion of Jeffers, turned against him. "The book as a whole reveals no new juxtaposition of the parts of Jeffers' hybrid nature," says a reviewer in the October 18, 1937, issue, "but rather a wearied division between them—with the aging prophet still hell-bent on emitting clouds of sulphur and smoke, and the poet simultaneously becoming more and more corner-loving and mealy-eyed."

The last thing people wanted to hear was that which many of them already believed: the world was moving toward another war. In a poem titled "Rearmament," Jeffers refers to the "grand and fatal" movement of the world toward death. He describes the "disastrous rhythm, the heavy and mobile masses, the dance of the/ Dream-led masses down the dark mountain." In "Hellenistics" he says, "The age darkens, Europe mixes her cups of death, all the little Caesars fidget on their thrones./ The old wound opens its clotted mouth to ask for new wounds." Meanwhile, people prepare to die and kill for faith. Is it any wonder, Jeffers asks in "The Purse-Seine," that the poetry of those living in a time of turmoil is "troubled or frowning," or that it becomes hysterical and breaks into "splintered gleams, crackled laughter?" "But they are quite wrong," he asserts. "There is no reason for amazement: surely one always knew that cultures decay, and life's end is death."

Though Jeffers faced the end of Western civilization with equanimity, the road toward that end, lined with horrors, troubled him, as did the approach of his own death and worse, the decline of his career. The poet turned fifty in 1937. He received an honorary doctorate from Occidental College that year and he was elected to membership in the National Institute of Arts and Letters, but such recognition, welcome as it was, helped to reaffirm his sense of growing old. It was in 1937, too, that Jeffers sifted through his entire life's work, choosing poems for a major retrospective text.

The Selected Poetry of Robinson Jeffers appeared at the end of 1938. In the spring of that year, with his work on the book almost concluded, Jeffers left a farewell note to Una on his desk. Prior to leaving on a plane trip with his brother, Jeffers had a premonition that he would die. No doubt the destination, Death Valley, and the date, Easter, helped loosen subconscious fears.

> On account of a dream I had in London—for no one knows what previsions the human mind is capable of—and a 'hunch' I have here, it seems possible that we may crash on the way to Death Valley in spite of Hamilton's flying experience. Therefore this note and the enclosed holograph last will and testament. But a 'hunch' is not an assurance; I wouldn't bet money on a 'hunch' and it would be just cowardly to refuse an air-plane ride for one. I say this to avoid misunderstanding because I have no desire to die before writing another poem or two and I should love to know you and the boys for hundreds of years to come, and the beauty of things.
>
> Aside from these considerations I have no prejudice against dying at any time—no desire to but also no shrinking from it so you are not to mourn me if it should happen, but remember that I loved you dearly and wanted you and the boys to be happy,— not sorrowful. Remember also that it is vulgar for poor people to spend money on funerals. I wish to be cremated as cheaply, quickly and quietly as possible, no speech nor meeting nor music,

no more coffin than may be necessary, no embalming, no flowers. A funeral is only a sanitary measure. Put the ashes a few inches deep in the courtyard near our little daughter's ashes—certainly no gravestone nor tablet.

As to the proposed 'Selected'—in case what I imagine should happen—'*Collected* Poems' go ahead with them. I trust your judgment more than I do my own. I will try to get the preface done more or less, and to copy legibly the two or three bits of recent verse that might be added. I really think that the poems are valuable and memorable but how should I know? Don't forget the dedication to U. J. I will copy it out legibly. Finally my dearest love to you and our boys. More than I have ever been able to express (SL 265).

Jeffers returned home safely. In June, however, when he journeyed with his family to Taos, he still suffered from feelings of despair. Sara Bard Field, a close friend, did not want Robinson and Una to go to New Mexico that year. She disliked Mabel, especially for the way she interfered with people's lives. "Don't do it," she told Una, "you'll regret it in time" (SBF 487). As it turned out, her fears were justified.

Disciple of Lawrence that she was, Mabel decided that Jeffers should have an affair. Only the passionate embrace of a younger woman, she believed, could revivify his spirits and restore the flow of creative energy within. Fortunately, she had the perfect candidate on hand: a woman named Hildegarde, soon to be called by Una "the snake." Hildegarde had arrived at Mabel's as a refugee from a troubled marriage. Her husband, a university press editor, had recently returned home with his mistress, hoping to live in a *ménage a trois*.

Jeffers either pursued the woman or surrendered to her charms. Mabel helped by finding places for their trysts (which might have included nothing more than deep conversations) and, no doubt, by keeping Una busy while the two were off alone.

Una was devastated when she found out what was going on. Intensely jealous anyway, she felt embarrassed and betrayed. She went upstairs, took Robinson's .32 revolver from a drawer, went into the bathroom, and, to avoid spilling blood on the floor, lay down in the tub. She then placed the gun beneath her left breast, aimed the barrel at her heart, and pulled the trigger. The bullet was deflected by a rib. Instead of passing straight through her body, it traveled beneath her skin around her side and exited from her back. Though the wound was serious, she survived.

After about a week in the hospital, Una prepared for the journey home. After she and Robinson left that year, they never vacationed in Taos again.

Back in Carmel, Una was unstable for a while. She cried frequently and withdrew into herself. But with Robinson's help, she soon recovered her emotional and physical strength. The comforting rhythm of life at Tor House restored her and signs of trauma quickly disappeared. "As for my wound," she says in a letter to a friend, written a few months later, "it's all right. It makes a thrilling scar and gives me no trouble but wasn't that an awkward thing to happen" (RJN #51).

In time, the events at Taos were remembered by Robinson and Una as if they had occurred in a bad dream.

Even so, Jeffers continued to suffer from an inability to write. Una tried to help her husband by writing to a friend who owned a home nearby; there was a guest house on the property and Una asked if Robinson could rent it for awhile. "He is working at something which needs a new set-up (maybe)," she says. "After all he has worked at the same table now for twenty years. He sometimes feels that a change of position might be useful and visualized a bare room with nothing in it but a table & chair & bare walls where he could be quiet & hidden & unseen." The friend was more than happy to make the arrangements but Una wrote again, in October, and said that Robinson no longer wanted to move (RJN #51).

The Selected Poetry of Robinson Jeffers appeared in December 1938. Among the handful of reviews the six-hundred-page distillation of his life's work received, none was more curt than *Time* magazine's five-sentence denunciation. "For the most part," the author says in the December 26, 1938, issue, Jeffers fills his empty world "with mythological personages, semi-scientific platitudes, nonpoetical intensities, and—for the pay-off—mental exhaustion. . . . Because his words are impersonally grandiose instead of personally grand, Robinson Jeffers, who in another place and another time might have been a prophet, is here and now a vasty poetaster."

Though comments such as these no doubt stung, Jeffers had long since abandoned the hope of pleasing every reader. Addressing himself in a poem titled "The Great Sunset," he says "'To be truth-bound, the neutral / Detested by all the dreaming factions, is my errand here.'"

Jeffers regarded fame as a long creance, the cord that keeps a falcon tied to its master's wrist. Artists, he says in "Let Them Alone," a poem written late in his career, should be free.

> *A poet is one who listens*
> *To nature and his own heart; and if the noise of the world grows up*
> *   around him, and if he is tough enough,*
> *He can shake off his enemies but not his friends.*
> *That is what withered Wordsworth and muffled Tennyson, and*
> *   would have killed Keats; that is what makes*
> *Hemingway play the fool and Faulkner forget his art.*

The sirens of success still sang to Jeffers—in 1939 he was given an honorary doctorate from the University of Southern California and in 1940 he accepted an invitation from the Library of Congress in Washington, D.C. to inaugurate a poetry series—but he did not really hear them. What he heard when he listened to nature, his own heart, and the noise of the world around him, he says in "Dawn," was the sound of pain: "what an ass life looks. / High on the dawn the enormous angular shadow of a sick ass being clubbed to death."

Just as World War I intensified his experience of life and concentrated his energy as a poet, World War II provided the impetus Jeffers needed to write. This time, however, there was a difference. His muse, once a young and graceful maiden, passionate and untamed, had become bitter and old. As in Greek mythology, where Artemis turns into Hecate the crone, the archetypal feminine force at work in Jeffers wrapped herself in black, left the

mountainside, and journeyed underground—where the Furies
are and the Harpies and doglike Hecuba. She still inspired him
to speak of God, but in darker, more mournful tones.

> Dear God, who are the whole splendor of things and the sacred
>   stars, but also the cruelty and greed, the treacheries
> And vileness, insanities and filth and anguish: now that this thing
>   comes near us again I am finding it hard
> To praise you with a whole heart.
>   I know what pain is, but pain can
>   shine. I know what death is, I have sometimes
> Longed for it. But cruelty and slavery and degradation, pestilence,
>   filth, the pitifulness
> Of men like little hurt birds and animals . . . if you were only
> Waves beating rock, the wind and the iron-cored earth, the flaming
>   insolent wildness of sun and stars,
> With what a heart I could praise your beauty.
>   You will not repent, nor cancel life, nor
>   free man from anguish
> For many ages to come. You are the one that tortures himself to dis-
>   cover himself: I am
> One that watches you and discovers you, and praises you in little
>   parables, idyl or tragedy, beautiful
> Intolerable God.

These lines are found in "Contemplation of the Sword," a poem
that appeared in *Be Angry at the Sun*, published in 1941.

In the same year, *The Tower Beyond Tragedy* was performed
by a local company. Judith Anderson, the noted actress and a
friend of the Jeffers family, played the role of Clytemnestra.
Jeffers saw the play three nights out of four and was deeply
moved, especially by Anderson's powerful performance. Four
years later, when she asked him to adapt Euripides' *Medea* for
the modern stage, with her in mind for the title role, he agreed,
much to Una's surprise. "He has never been able to bend his
mind immediately to suggestions for themes," she says, "but
Medea interested him" and a script was ready in a few months'
time (SMT 194).

Medea interested Jeffers for a variety of reasons, not the least of which was his apparent identification with Euripides. Throughout his career he had borrowed from all three major Greek dramatists—Aeschylus, Sophocles, and Euripides—but at this moment in his life he no doubt felt closest to the latter. It was Euripides, after all, who was noted for his solitariness, for his antagonism toward war, and for his plays about violent women. An essay by Jeffers written about Euripides to supplement his adaptation of the play could have been written about himself. Change "Greece" to "Western civilization" and change "Athens" to "America" in the following paragraph, where Jeffers is discussing reasons why contemporaries of Euripides did not like him, and the similarities are easy to see.

> There were other counts against Euripides. His great precursors were more than poets and play-wrights; they were also exemplary citizens. Aeschylus had fought at Marathon, that day of glory; Sophocles had taken an admired part in civic affairs, and was appointed a general of the army. But Euripides remained a private man, a disillusioned student and man of letters. The world had changed in his time, the great dream was fading. Recently Athens had been the savior of all Greece; but now Greece had fallen apart, and Athens, though grown much greater, was only an imperialistic power struggling with Sparta for supremacy, busy with confused battles and oppressions. Therefore, as many honest men have done since his time, Euripides chose to stay aloof from public life; and it seems to me that he was right in his time; but his fellow-citizens judged otherwise (SMT 217).

Medea also interested Jeffers for the story that it told. The play is about a sorceress who helped her lover, Jason, obtain the Golden Fleece. After further adventures, the two settle in Corinth and have two sons. No longer needing her, Jason abandons Medea when the king of Corinth offers him his daughter as a wife. Medea, not one to be betrayed, calls on Hecate for help with her revenge. She sends a wedding gift: a beautiful cape that kills the king's daughter as soon as she puts it on and kills the king himself when he tries to save her. Still filled with contempt for Jason and wanting to hurt him more, Medea murders their two children. She then flees Corinth, leaving Jason broken and alone.

Jeffers' adaptation of the play opened on Broadway in October 1947. Anderson played the title role and John Gielgud performed the part of Jason. Had the audience known the darkness in Jeffers' soul from which his portrait of Medea emerged or had it fully understood the relevance of the play for modern times, where Medea represented the hate-filled violence of a war that had just claimed millions of innocent lives, the people might have run for the theater doors. But Anderson held the audience spellbound. Almost everyone agreed that Jeffers' adaptation of the play was brilliant and Anderson's performance astonishing. In a review dated October 21, 1947, Brooks Atkinson of the *New York Times* called their work a landmark of the modern stage.

The play ran from October to May, for a total of 214 successful performances. A national touring company was then formed and independent productions were planned for Denmark, Italy, France, Germany, England, and other places around the world.

If *Medea* expressed Jeffers' feelings about the war in a symbolic way and thus obscured them, his next book revealed exactly where he stood. *The Double Axe* appeared in 1948. Poems contained therein, written throughout the war, were so virulent, so gruesome in places, so much against America, civilization, and humanity as a whole, that Random House felt compelled to disassociate itself from them. In a highly unusual move, perhaps unprecedented, the company prefaced the collection with a "Publisher's Note" in which it went on record with "its disagreement over some of the political views pronounced by the poet in this volume."

The book was, in fact, an unmediated howl of outrage and pain. The opening poem, "The Love and the Hate," is about a young soldier, recently killed in battle, who returns home to haunt his patriot father and adulterous mother. At one point, with his dead body still intact, the boy forces his mother to stick her hand into a hole blown open in his chest. In "Moments of Glory," Jeffers condemns Churchill, Hitler, and Truman as equally contemptible men. And in "Orca," he says "the earth is a star" and the "human element/Is what darkens it."

Jeffers knew who he was or what he had become. In "Cassandra," another poem published in *The Double Axe,* he sees himself in a character he had brought to life many years before: "The mad girl with the staring eyes and long white fingers/ Hooked in the stones of the wall,/The storm-wrack hair and the screeching mouth." Poor bitch, he says to his alter ego, be wise, be quiet. "No: you'll still mumble in a corner a crust of truth, to men/And gods disgusting.—You and I, Cassandra."

Robinson and Una were in Ireland when *The Double Axe* appeared. They arrived June 10, 1948, with plans to explore their beloved British Isles for the next few months. By the middle of July, however, Robinson was in the hospital, first in Kilkenny and then Dublin. He contracted a strep infection of the pleural cavity with encroachment on the heart, a life-threatening condition that caused tremendous pain. August 2, the thirty-fifth anniversary of Robinson's and Una's marriage, found Jeffers better but far from being cured. Treatment continued for the next few weeks until, on September 4, the doctor believed he was draining Jeffers' pleural cavity for the last time. On that day, however, an air embolism occurred, moved through the bloodstream to Jeffers' brain, and almost killed him. Heart stimulants, artificial respiration, and other emergency techniques, frantically applied, brought Jeffers through the crisis, but he was delirious for the next two days. Finally, on September 20, he was well enough to leave the hospital and return home.

When Robinson and Una arrived in San Francisco, they were met by Donnan, his wife Lee, and their son Lindsay. With a tremendous feeling of relief, says Una in her diary, they bundled into the car and started for Carmel. The sun was shining and California looked beautiful.

Tor House awaited us with flag flying from the top of the tower. (Donnan had hoisted it before dawn.) *A great surprise*. A little plot of lawn by the sun dial, and shellpath in the courtyard and big beds of flowers in bloom. How they worked to accomplish this. The house was spick and span. Robin climbed happily into bed, and looked out over our wonderful rocks with great waves foaming over them. Lindsay was already laughing and playing with us . . . the lovely Rose-a-Lindsay. I felt as if a tractor had run over me several times, but I was very happy to get home again in my own dear place (SMT 213).

Una thought her troubles were over. Unfortunately, however, they had just begun. Robinson eventually recovered but her own fatigue never disappeared. In October she wrote to a friend and said, "I am very tired & find it hard to get my life in order again" (RJN #55). As fall progressed, her symptoms worsened. By year's end, what was diagnosed as an obscure abdominal infection that induced lethargy, nausea, and a recurrent fever was serious enough to warrant exploratory surgery.

The operation took place in January 1949. Adhesions believed to be from an earlier operation were found to be inflamed. These were removed and the areas around them treated, but nearly a month passed before Una was well enough to go home.

Before long, other symptoms appeared. In addition to a general feeling of weakness, Una suffered from excruciating pain in her back and legs. Doctors treated her for sciatica but soon discovered there was little they could do to help her. In 1941 Una had had a breast removed. From 1941 to 1944 she underwent therapy for cancer. Now, after a remission of five years, the cancer was back, having spread throughout her spine. There was talk of cutting Una's sciatic nerve, which would have left her paralyzed, or of giving her a lobotomy, which would have left her mentally numb, but both plans were dismissed. Radiation and experimental hormones were given, along with morphine. Eventually, only the morphine was necessary.

Una's death was slow in coming. She lived through 1949 and most of 1950, never once allowing the disease to break her spirit. Her biggest concern was for her family. As she says in a letter to Judith Anderson, dated June 28, 1950, "more distressing to me than my own pain in my sickness has been the anxiety I've caused Robin and the children and the disruption of our regular life" (RJN #65).

Late in August, Robinson wrote one of Una's sisters to say that Una was as happy as possible at Tor House, the only place she ever wanted to be. "Una has a sweet room," he says. It looks "down on the ocean and rock-islands covered with birds, gulls, pelicans and cormorants; and the sea-lions passing; and the land-birds, quail and the singing sparrows and linnets, in the bushes under the window." "Her favorite books are on the walls or near by," he adds, along with flowers and other gifts from friends. "I am sure that Una feels how important and how much loved she is. But she refuses (usually) to see anyone," except for members of the family (SL 326). Eventually, she had to be moved to the hospital in Carmel, but Robinson was with her, as he had been from the beginning. On September 1, 1950, she died in his arms.

Throughout this difficult period, Jeffers was fortunate to have his son Donnan and his daughter-in-law Lee beside him. After residing in Ohio for a while, Donnan returned to Carmel and worked as an accountant. He and Lee lived at Tor House, where Lee's devotion as a homemaker and experience as a nurse proved invaluable. Jeffers' other son Garth and his wife Charlotte were living near Yosemite at this time. After serving as an M.P. in Germany during the war, he joined the National Forest Service. Degrees in anthropology and forestry enabled him to work in a special field division, one that identified sites formerly used by Native Americans and proposed logging policies that would leave them undisturbed.

Life went on for Robinson after Una's death, but without much savor. "Una has died," he says in "Hungerfield," a poem written a year later, "and I/ Am left waiting for death, like a leafless tree/ Waiting for the roots to rot and the trunk to fall." As he waited, the recollection of Una's suffering was difficult to bear. "This is my wound. This is what never time nor change nor whiskey will heal:/ To have watched the bladed throat-muscles lifting the breast-bone, frail strands of exhausted flesh, laboring, laboring/Only for a little air." He knew, as he had always known but all the more deeply now, that "poets who sing of life without remembering its agony/ Are fools or liars."

The passage of time did not heal the wound nor did alcohol dull the pain—not even a bottle of whiskey a day along with three gallons of wine a week. As he writes in a privately printed poem, "Whom Should I Write For, Dear, But For You?", another turn of the seasons found him right where he had been.

Whom should I write for, dear, but for you? Two years have passed,
The wound is bleeding—new and will never heal.
I used to write for you, and give you the poem
When it was written, and wait uneasily your verdict . . . but now, to
whom?

—As for you,
You have a better life than to read my verses.
You have gone up with the flame to the high air; and that pitiful
bone-ash,
Not buried deeply, lives in bright flowers
In the garden you loved.—As for the precious human consciousness—
(Yours was most precious to me, not mine, nor theirs)
I think it is taken into the great dream of the earth; for this dark
planet
Has its own consciousness, from which yours came,
And now returns: as the earth's consciousness,
Half-separate for a time, will return at length
To the whole galaxy; and when that perishes
To the whole endless universe—that is, to God,
Who will make all things new.

But for me, here, the momentary loneliness
Is hard to bear.

Though troubled, Jeffers was not constantly depressed. He continued to write in the mornings and he helped his son work on the house in the afternoons. Donnan inherited his father's love for stonemasonry and slowly expanded Tor House until it was over three times its original size. Jeffers also had Lee for companionship, visits from Garth and Charlotte to look forward to, dogs to walk, and grandchildren to enjoy. And he had his sense of humor (which, throughout his life, had been exceedingly dry). One night during this time, after a dinner that included oysters from the East Coast sent to the Jefferses by friends, Lee found Robinson carefully disposing of the shells. As she tells the story, he was placing them in an area once used by Indians for their abalone feasts. "What are you doing?" she asked politely. "I'm putting these here to confuse future archaeologists," he replied, smiling.

Jeffers' next book of poems, *Hungerfield*, appeared in 1954. The title poem, addressed to Una, is about a man who wrestles with Death in order to save his mother's life. The book also contains an adaptation of *Hippolytus*, another play by Euripides, which Jeffers calls *The Cretan Woman*. This play contains the last lines in Jeffers' work spoken directly by a goddess. Aphrodite ends the play with some advice to people. Lest they become too proud, too self-satisfied, too removed from the harsh realities of life (including love), they should remember: "Something is lurking hidden./ There is always a knife in the flowers. There is always a lion just beyond the firelight."

Hungerfield also contains a number of short lyric poems that restate Jeffers' philosophy of life or reaffirm his poetic values. The task of the artist, he says in "The Beauty of Things," is "to feel and speak the astonishing beauty of things—earth, stone and water,/ Beast, man and woman, sun, moon and stars—/ The blood-shot beauty of human nature, its thoughts, frenzies and passions,/ And unhuman nature its towering reality." Anything else in art is simply diversion.

A few years before the publication of *Hungerfield*, Jeffers wrote an essay for the January 18, 1948, edition of the *New York Times Magazine* which makes the same case. In "Poetry, Gongorism and a Thousand Years," he says that poetry should be "natural and direct" and come from "a man's mind and senses and bloodstream." It should also reflect a certain detachment: "it is not necessary, because each epoch is confused, that its poet should share its confusion." And most important, poetry should deal with the "permanent" aspects of life. As Jeffers argued throughout his career, poetry should be sifted of that which is "transient and crumbling, the chaff of time and the stuff that requires footnotes." A great poet, Jeffers concludes, writes with posterity in mind. He avoids the "doctrinaire corruptions of instinct" that establish fashion for an age and attempts to speak clearly to an audience a thousand years away. "If the present time overhears him, and listens too—all the better," but he should not seek fame in his lifetime. "To be peered at and interviewed, to be pursued by idlers and autograph hunters and inquiring admirers, would surely be a sad nuisance. And it is destructive too, if you take it seriously; it wastes your energy into self-consciousness; it destroys spontaneity and soils the springs of the mind. Whereas posthumous reputation could do you no harm at all, and is really the only kind worth considering."

As far as Jeffers himself was concerned, critics were happy to oblige. Though he continued to receive recognition for his work, including a $5,000 award from the Academy of American Poets, fewer and fewer serious readers paid attention to him. Kenneth Rexroth describes the decline of Jeffers' reputation in an essay written for the *Saturday Review*, August 10, 1957. "In recent years," Rexroth says, "the stock of Robinson Jeffers has fallen; for an entire literary generation it might be said to have plummeted and still be plummeting." "Today," he adds, "young people simply do not read him. Few young poets of my acquaintance, and I know most of them, have ever opened one of his books, and know only the anthology pieces, which, I am afraid, they dislike." For Rexroth, this situation was fine.

> In my opinion, Jeffers's verse is shoddy and pretentious and the philosophizing is nothing but posturing. His reworkings of Greek tragic plots make me shudder at their vulgarity, the coarsening of sensibility, the cheapening of the language, and the tawdriness of the paltry insight into the great ancient meanings. His lyrics and reveries of the Californian landscape seem to me to suffer in almost every line from the most childish laboring of the pathetic fallacy, elevated to a very system of response.... His philosophy I find a mass of contradictions—high-flown statements indulged in for their melodrama alone, and often essentially meaningless.

In short, says Rexroth, there is nothing in Jeffers' work but "fustian and rodomontade."

For Rexroth, the decline of Jeffers' reputation began in 1932 when Yvor Winters wrote the review that appeared in *Hound & Horn*, the review that contained, he believed, "one of the most devastating attacks" against a poet in modern criticism. In truth, however, no one critic deserves the credit or the blame. Literary opinion mid-century was shaped by many people, most of whom found it difficult to read Jeffers' work. Except for toss-away comments like R. P. Blackmur's reference to "the flannel-mouthed inflation" of Jeffers' metrical schemes (in an essay published in *The Kenyon Review*, Winter 1952), the influential New Critics completely ignored him. In 1973, for instance, Cleanth Brooks, R. W. B. Lewis, and Robert Penn Warren published their two-volume, four-thousand-page anthology of American literature titled *American Literature: The Makers and the Making*. The book introduces the major and minor writers who lived between 1620 and 1970 and includes selections from their work. Jeffers does not appear in the anthology, nor is he mentioned, not even in a footnote.

Lack of immediate attention did not bother him. As he says in his *Times* essay, "I have no sympathy with the notion that the world owes a duty to poetry, or any other art. Poetry is not a civilizer, rather the reverse, for great poetry appeals to the most primitive instincts. It is not necessarily a moralizer; it does not necessarily improve one's character; it does not even teach good manners. It is a beautiful work of nature, like an eagle or a high sunrise. You owe it no duty. If you like it, listen to it; if not, let it alone." Besides, he knew his poetry was often filled with violence and pain and thus was not for everybody. He also knew, however, that his poetry, like his granite home, was exceptionally well built and strong enough to stand the test of time.

Hungerfield was the last of his books of poems that Jeffers saw published. His health began to fail after it appeared. Years of heavy smoking left his lungs weak; hardening of the arteries left his limbs cold; a cataract left him nearly blind. One eye was good for "common daylight," he says, while the other saw "gods and spirits in its cloud / And the weird end of the world" (SMT 236). At seventy-five he walked with a stoop, as his father had.

Eventually, he was confined to bed—the same bed Una used when she was dying, the one downstairs where they made love before going up to sleep so many years before. He lay there tapping with his hand at times, as if working with stone or scanning the rhythm of a poem. Occasionally, he moaned. Above him was a line from Spenser's *Faerie Queene*: "Sleepe after toyle, port after stormie seas, / Ease after warre, death after life does greatly please."

The line had been inscribed on a beam soon after Tor House was built, just as the bed had been readied with its present purpose in mind. The bed is described in a poem titled "The Bed by the Window," written early in Jeffers' career.

I chose the bed down-stairs by the sea-window for a good death-bed
When we built the house; it is ready waiting,
Unused unless by some guest in a twelvemonth, who hardly suspects
Its latter purpose. I often regard it,
With neither dislike nor desire; rather with both, so equalled
That they kill each other and a crystalline interest
Remains alone. We are safe to finish what we have to finish;
And then it will sound rather like music
When the patient daemon behind the screen of sea-rock and sky
Thumps with his staff, and calls thrice: 'Come, Jeffers.'

On January 20, 1962, it was time. There was no funeral, no memorial service of any kind. Jeffers was cremated. His children buried the ashes where Una's were buried twelve years before—beneath a yew tree in the courtyard of Tor House.

Conclusion

On the little stone-girdled platform
Over the earth and the ocean
I seem to have stood a long time and watched the stars pass.

These lines, which appear in a poem titled "Margrave," bring us back to where we started—the turret of Hawk Tower. If you stand there when day turns into night, you can watch the sun drop slowly through the sky and touch the ocean. You half expect to see the water hiss and steam, but nothing happens. The sun sinks coolly beneath the waves. Sometimes the sky is streaked with brilliant orange and the clouds appear to glow, as if from the banked heat of inner fire; but the fire soon fades and the clouds, like heaps of ashes, turn gray and cold. Darkness comes and then the stars appear. "They also shall perish," continues "Margrave," "Here to-day, gone to-morrow, desperate wee galaxies / Scattering themselves and shining their substance away / Like a passionate thought." That's all anything can do— stars, flowers, or people. We are earth, air, and water, said Heraclitus, held together and consumed by "ever-living Fire."

Life is "a torch to burn in with pride," says Jeffers in *Cawdor*; it is "a necessary / Ecstasy in the run of the cold substance." We break the somnambulism of nature, catch the beauty of things in a net of nerves, and then we pass away. His poem titled "Inscription for a Gravestone" suggests this epitaph:

I admired the beauty
While I was human, now I am part of the beauty.
I wander in the air,
Being mostly gas and water, and flow in the ocean;
Touch you and Asia
At the same moment; have a hand in the sunrises
And the glow of this grass.
I left the light precipitate of ashes to earth
For a love-token.

Jeffers left more than ashes. He left his home, which he intended to inhabit for ages. Visit in ten thousand years, he says in "Tor House," and you will find his spirit dwelling on his hill above the ocean. Even if the structure has fallen into ruin, he adds in "Post Mortem," some of the rocks he handled will remain, and he will still be in them—as a dark ghost, a "long sunset shadow in the seams of the granite . . . a spirit for the stone."

Jeffers also left his poetry, which he expected to endure. It is a curious fact, he says, that "flower-soft verse/ Is sometimes harder than granite, tougher than a steel cable, more alive than life" (CP III 477).

But even if his poems fall from human consciousness, Jeffers believed the message they contain will remain forever valid. In a poem titled "Going to Horse Flats," which tells the story of an encounter with a hermit on a wilderness trail, Jeffers reaffirms his confidence in the ideas that shaped his life and inspired his work for more than forty years.

Sweet was the clear
Chatter of the stream now that our talk was hushed; the flitting
water-ouzel returned to her stone;
A lovely snake, two delicate scarlet lines down the dark back, swam
through the pool. The flood-battered
Trees by the stream are more noble than cathedral-columns.

Why do we
invite the world's rancors and agonies

Into our minds though walking in a wilderness? Why did he want
    the news of the world? He could do nothing
To help nor hinder. Nor you nor I can . . . for the world. It is cer-
    tain the world cannot be stopped nor saved.
It has changes to accomplish and must creep through agonies toward
    new discovery. It must, and it ought: the awful necessity
Is also the sacrificial duty. Man's world is a tragic music and is not
    played for man's happiness,
Its discords are not resolved but by other discords.

                    But for each man
There is real solution, let him turn from himself and man to love
    God. He is out of the trap then. He will remain
Part of the music, but will hear it as the player hears it.
He will be superior to death and fortune, unmoved by success or
    failure. Pity can make him weep still,
Or pain convulse him, but not to the center, and he can conquer
    them . . . . But how could I impart this knowledge
To that old man?

                        Or indeed to anyone? I know that all
    men instinctively rebel against it. But yet
They will come to it at last.

Spring Storm, Portuguese Ridge, Sur Coast, 1971 *(Morley Baer)*

Bibliography

Major Publications By Jeffers

Flagons and Apples. Los Angeles: Grafton Publishing Company, 1912; reprinted Cayucos Books, 1970.

Californians. New York: The Macmillan Company, 1916; reprinted Cayucos Books, 1971.

Tamar and Other Poems. New York: Peter G. Boyle, 1924.

Roan Stallion, Tamar and Other Poems. New York: Boni & Liveright, 1925.

The Women at Point Sur. New York: Boni & Liveright, 1927; reprinted New York: Liveright, 1977.

Cawdor and Other Poems. New York: Horace Liveright, 1928.

Dear Judas and Other Poems. New York: Horace Liveright, 1929; reprinted New York: Liveright, 1977.

Descent to the Dead. New York: Random House, 1931.

Thurso's Landing and Other Poems. New York: Liveright, Inc., Publishers, 1932.

Give Your Heart to the Hawks and Other Poems. New York: Random House, 1933.

Solstice and Other Poems. New York: Random House, 1935.

Such Counsels You Gave to Me and Other Poems. New York: Random House, 1937.

The Selected Poetry of Robinson Jeffers. New York: Random House, 1938.

Be Angry at the Sun. New York: Random House, 1941.

Medea, Freely Adapted from the Medea of Euripides. New York: Random House, 1946.

The Double Axe and Other Poems. New York: Random House, 1948; reprinted New York: Liveright, 1977.

Hungerfield and Other Poems. New York: Random House, 1954.

The Beginning and the End and Other Poems. New York: Random House, 1963.

Robinson Jeffers: Selected Poems. New York: Vintage Books, 1965.

The Alpine Christ and Other Poems. Edited by William Everson. Cayucos Books, 1974.

Brides of the South Wind: Poems 1917-1922. Edited by William Everson. Cayucos Books, 1974.

Rock and Hawk: A Selection of Shorter Poems by Robinson Jeffers. Edited by Robert Hass. New York: Random House, 1987.

The Collected Poetry of Robinson Jeffers. 4 Volumes. Edited by Tim Hunt. Stanford: Stanford University Press, 1988.

Secondary Sources

Adamic, Louis. *Robinson Jeffers: A Portrait*. Seattle: University of Washington Bookstore, 1929; reprinted Covelo, California: The Yolla Bolly Press, 1983.

Alberts, Sidney S. *A Bibliography of the Works of Robinson Jeffers*. New York: Random House, 1933; reprinted Rye, New York: Cultural History Resource, 1966.

Benediktsson, Thomas. *George Sterling*. Boston: Twayne Publishers, 1980.

Bennett, Melba Berry. *The Stone Mason of Tor House: The Life and Work of Robinson Jeffers*. Los Angeles: The Ward Ritchie Press, 1966.

Brooks, Van Wyck. *An Autobiography*. New York: E. P. Dutton & Co., 1965; reprinted Hamden, Connecticut: The Shoe String Press, 1976.

Brophy, Robert. *Robinson Jeffers: Myth, Ritual, and Symbol in His Narrative Poems*. Cleveland: Case Western Reserve University

Press, 1973; reprinted Hamden, Connecticut: The Shoe String Press, 1976.

Cerf, Bennett. *At Random: The Reminiscences of Bennett Cerf.* New York: Random House, 1977.

deFord, Miriam Allen. *They Were San Franciscans.* Caldwell, Idaho: The Caxton Printers, 1941.

Field, Sara Bard. *Sara Bard Field: Poet and Suffragist.* An interview conducted by Amelia R. Fry. Berkeley, California: Regional Oral History Office, The Bancroft Library, University of California, 1979.

Freeman, Kathleen. *Ancilla to the Pre-Socratic Philosophers.* Cambridge: Harvard University Press, 1971.

Greenan, Edith. *Of Una Jeffers.* Los Angeles: The Ward Ritchie Press, 1939.

Jeffers, Donnan. "Some Notes on the Building of Tor House" and "The Stones of Tor House." Privately printed.

Jeffers, Robinson, and Lyon, Horace. *Jeffers Country: The Seed Plots of Robinson Jeffers' Poetry.* San Francisco: The Scrimshaw Press, 1971.

Jeffers, Robinson. *The Selected Letters of Robinson Jeffers, 1897-1962.* Edited by Ann N. Ridgeway. Baltimore: The Johns Hopkins Press, 1968.

Jeffers, Robinson. *"What Odd Expedients" and Other Poems by Robinson Jeffers.* Edited by Robert Ian Scott. Hamden, Connecticut: The Shoe String Press, 1981.

Jeffers, Robinson and Una. *Where Shall I Take You To: The Love Letters of Una and Robinson Jeffers.* Edited by Robert Kafka. Covelo, California: The Yolla Bolly Press, 1987.

Karman, James, ed. *Critical Essays on Robinson Jeffers.* Boston: G. K. Hall & Co., 1990.

Kuster, Una. "The Enduring Element of Mysticism in Man." University of Southern California, 1910.

Luhan, Mabel Dodge. *Lorenzo in Taos.* New York: Alfred A. Knopf, 1932.

Luhan, Mabel Dodge. *Una and Robin.* University of California: The Friends of the Bancroft Library, 1976.

Moore, Harry T. *The Priest of Love: A Life of D. H. Lawrence*. New York: Farrar, Straus and Giroux, 1974.

Noel, Joseph. *Footloose in Arcadia: A Personal Record of Jack London, George Sterling, Ambrose Bierce*. New York: Carrick & Evans, 1940.

Not Man Apart: Lines from Robinson Jeffers, Photographs of the Big Sur Coast. Edited by David Brower. New York: Ballantine Books, 1969.

Powell, Lawrence Clark. *Robinson Jeffers: The Man and His Work*. Pasadena, California: San Pasqual Press, 1940.

Robinson Jeffers Newsletter. Edited by Robert J. Brophy. Published quarterly by California State University, Long Beach University Press.

Rudnick, Lois Palken. *Mabel Dodge Luhan: New Woman, New Worlds*. Albuquerque: University of New Mexico Press, 1984.

St. Johns, Adela Rogers. *Final Verdict*. Garden City, New York: Doubleday, 1962.

Serra, Junípero. *Writings of Junípero Serra*, Volume II. Edited by Antonine Tibesar, O. F. M. Washington, D. C.: Academy of American Franciscan History, 1956.

Shebl, James. *In This Wild Water: The Suppressed Poems of Robinson Jeffers*. Pasadena, California: Ward Ritchie Press, 1976.

Starr, Kevin. *Americans and the California Dream, 1850—1915*. New York: Oxford University Press, 1973.

Sterling, George. *Robinson Jeffers: The Man and the Artist*. New York: Boni & Liveright, 1926.

Vardamis, Alex A. *The Critical Reputation of Robinson Jeffers: A Bibliographical Study*. Hamden, Connecticut: Archon Books, 1972.

Walker, Franklin. *The Seacoast of Bohemia*. Santa Barbara, California: Peregrine Smith, 1973.

Weston, Edward. *The Daybooks of Edward Weston: California*. Edited by Nancy Newhall. New York: Horizon Press, 1966.

Weston, Jessie L. *From Ritual to Romance*. Garden City, New York: Doubleday Anchor Books, 1957.

Winters, Yvor. *In Defense of Reason*. Denver: Alan Swallow, 1937.

Zaller, Robert. *The Cliffs of Solitude: A Reading of Robinson Jeffers*. Cambridge: Cambridge University Press, 1983.

Abbreviations

Index

Hippolytus/Phaedra story (Greek mythology), Jeffers' retellings of, 89–90, 142
Holy Grail, legend of the, 68
"Hooded Night," 103
Hopper, Jimmy, 26, 35–36, 39–40, 70, 76
Hopper, Mattie, 35, 39
Hughes, Langston, 125, 126
Humanism, 4, 41, 84–85, 99–100
Humanity (see also Civilization); Jeffers' condemnation of, 94–97
Hungerfield, 142, 144
"Hungerfield," 140
Hutchison, Percy A., 84, 122

Iconoclasm, 5
Idyls (Idyll) (literary form), 30, 37
Imagery, in Eliot's The Waste Land, 5
Imagination, Jeffers,' 42, 90; as diversion in childhood, 10–11
Incest, Jeffers' dramatic use of, 65, 66, 96–97, 121, 130
In Defense of Reason (Winters), 123–24
Indians (Native Americans), 82, 86–87; languages, 35
"Inhumanism," Jeffers' position defined as, 84–85
"Inscription for a Gravestone," 146–47
Introversion, human, incest as symbol for in Tamar, 66
"Invocation," 3–4
Irish culture, Una's interest in, 119–20

Jeffers, Annie Robinson Tuttle (mother), 8–9, 17, 21–22, 33, 36–37; death, 68–69; on family trips to Europe, 9–10, 11–12, 15–16
Jeffers, Barbara (grandmother), 7
Jeffers, Charlotte (daughter-in-law), 140, 141
Jeffers, Donnan (son), 112, 138, 140, 141, 145; birth, 36–37, 47; childhood, 52, 76, 108–9, 117, 118–19
Jeffers, Garth (son), 112, 140, 141, 145; birth, 36–37, 47; childhood, 52, 76, 108–9, 117, 118–19
Jeffers, Hamilton (brother), 11, 131

Jeffers, Joseph (grandfather), 7
Jeffers, Lee (daughter-in-law), 138, 140, 141
Jeffers, Lindsay (grandson), 138–39
Jeffers, Maeve (daughter), 23, 33
Jeffers, Robinson (John Robinson; Robin), 55, 58–59, 108–10, 112–13, 115–16
childhood and adolescence, 9–16, 17–18, 55
descriptions of, 30–32
education, 9–10, 11–12, 16–17, 34
following Una's death, 140–41; final days, 144–45
friendship with Sterling, 75–78
honorary degrees, 131, 134
inheritance, 34
life in California before marriage, 16–19; period of lassitude, 17–19; relationship with Una, 19, 21–22
lightning strike and transformation, 30, 32, 47–49, 63–65, 68
marriage to Una, 22–23
married life: birth and death of daughter, 23, 33; birth of sons, 36–37, 47; building of Tor House and Hawk Tower, 47–51; infidelity, 37, 132; life at Carmel cabin (1914–1919), 24–25, 29–30, 32–45; life at Tor House (1919–1925), 50–54, 63, 79–80; life at Tor House (following 1925), 117–20, 125–26, 129–30, 133; 1948 illness, 138–39; 1914 visit to Carmel, 23, 24; Una's impact on, 45–46; during Una's last illness and death, 138–40; visits to Taos and Mabel Dodge Luhan, 128–29, 132–33; during World War I, 38–39, 40–41
parents, 7–9 (see also Jeffers, Annie Robinson Tuttle; Jeffers, William Hamilton); influence, 14–15, 19, 34
works. See Poetry, of Robinson Jeffers; individual titles
Jeffers, Una Call Kuster (wife), xiii, 19–23, 48, 56–57, 59, 70, 108,